Faith, Love and Forgiveness

By: Misty Ballantyne

May 2014

Copyright © 2014 by Misty Ballantyne

Faith, Love and Forgiveness
by Misty Ballantyne

Printed in the United States of America

ISBN 9781498405324

All rights reserved solely by the author. The author guarantees all contents are original and do not infringe upon the legal rights of any other person or work. No part of this book may be reproduced in any form without the permission of the author. The views expressed in this book are not necessarily those of the publisher.

Scripture quotations taken from the English Standard Version (ESV). Copyright © 2012 by Crossway, a publishing ministry of Good News Publishers. Used by permission. All rights reserved.

www.xulonpress.com

Dedication

This book is dedicated to my loving husband, Earl and my three children, who are my world.

Acknowledgements

I would first of all like to thank my Lord and Savior, Jesus Christ for the inspiration and for His love, faithfulness and forgiveness that has been woven throughout my life. I would like to thank my family for all of their love and support, without it this endeavor would have been impossible. To my pastor, Jamey Collins, his wife Paula and their sweet family, and the Flat Rock Baptist church members who are so welcoming, loving and enthusiastically supportive. A very special thanks to a select few who read the story in its early stages and offered invaluable feedback. Lastly to my peeps, and you know who you are!! The encouragement and support you give is unparalleled, I love each and every one of you.

Special thanks to Lori Langston with Brownston Photography for the back cover photograph.

Table of Contents

Chapter 1   Ambiance of fall 11

Chapter 2   Family Tree 19

Chapter 3   Could this be love 26

Chapter 4   The Box 37

Chapter 5   Candy 48

Chapter 6   Boondoggle 58

Chapter 7   Halloween 68

Chapter 8   Driven 76

Chapter 9   Damages 83

Chapter 10 Mercy 95

Chapter 11 New Beginnings 108

Chapter 12 Dude 122

Chapter 13 The Invite 131

Chapter 14 Jet Set 142

Chapter 15 Home sweet home 153

Chapter 16 Your space or mine? 164

CHAPTER 1

Ambiance of fall

Ava Turner pulled into her parking space in the back lot of the downtown parking area reserved for store owners and employees. She loved this time of year when the air turned crisp and cool, but was not quite winter. The trees on the mountains are clothed in breath taking hues of canary yellow, ginger and bright red. She exited her vehicle and made her way to the breezeway that led to the stores on Main Street. The fall breeze sent fallen leaves scampering across the sidewalk in front of her as she walked toward the Caffeine Infusion Café, a store two doors down from her gift shop. She pulled her sweater up closer to her chin as she reached for the door handle.

The familiar door chime announced her arrival and she was greeted with a chorus of "Hello Ava" by the staff as she stepped inside. Instantly the aroma of freshly brewed coffee with blueberry muffins surrounded her and she smiled in spite of herself. Natasha was manning the counter this morning and Tim was wiping down a nearby table, both noticing Ava scanning the premises looking for Miles, the Café manager.

"He's in the store room, he'll be right back up." Natasha reassured.

"Oh? Sure that's fine, how are *you* this morning?" Ava said trying to sound nonchalant.

"I'm good. Do you want your regular?" She said as a smile spread across her tanned freckled face. Tim shot a look at his co-worker and grinned. Ava nodded her reply.

Natasha had watched this delicate dance between her gorgeous, incredibly kind boss Miles Petersen, and the lovely Christmas shop owner for the better part of two years now. They would chat for hours, go on "unofficial" dates and have lots of business meetings. Honestly, she wished they would just throw their arms around each other, profess undying love, kiss and put the rest of the spectators out of their misery. Apparently that is not how this is going to play out, but one could hope.

Carrying a load of coffee cups, filters and to go cups up from the basement storage area, Miles made his way up the steps and came in behind the counter. Seeing Ava standing at the counter awaiting her special hot chocolate, caused a huge smile to break out across his face. He set his load down and ran his hands through his wavy layered chestnut collar length hair.

"Hey, I'm so glad I didn't miss you." His smooth baritone voice softly filling the air.

Mesmerized by his hazel green eyes and winsome smile, Ava paused looking up at his six foot three inch frame that she never tired of the view. Realizing she was just standing there staring, shifting her weight to the other foot, and looking down at the counter she leaned in reaching for her sweet hot shot of caffeine. "Me too, I was running a little late this morning. I'm so relieved Maggie could open for me." She took a sip of her drink and thanked Natasha.

"Miles, I was wondering, what kind of day do you have planned?"

"Um, I've got some paperwork, a trip to the bank and dry cleaners. Nothing special. Why? Did you have something in mind?" Again unleashing that magnificent knee weakening smile.

"Well, I just wanted to get with you sometime soon to see if you have decided on your holiday theme for the Café this season. I have some wonderful ideas for your tree this year. That's all, nothing urgent. I just know we both get so busy during the fall season and I didn't want Christmas to sneak up on us."

She looked down to gently blow on her hot chocolate then lifted her eyes back up to look at him. Miles felt his pulse quicken and was acutely aware of the rapid beat of his heart as it pounded in his chest while he watched her from across the counter.

"What time are you closing the store tonight?" he stated leaning in and resting his elbows on the counter.

"Six. I should be finished by six o'clock. Will that work for you or is that getting into your evening crowd?"

"No, six is great. Michael and Katie will be here tonight and they can pretty much handle any crowd that shows up."

"Ok, I'll close up shop and head this way. See you then." She said flashing her own sweet smile.

Miles nodded and nearly melted into the counter as he watched her walk out the door and eventually out of view. Natasha walked passed him and swatted him with a bar towel, which snapped him back to reality. He turned, and grinned then began setting up the supplies he had brought from the store room.

Ava made her way back down the sidewalk admiring all the fall decorations and pumpkins that adorned many of the steps leading into the quaint shops located downtown. She floated into the La Noel Christmas store which had become her second home. Ava had taken over the store a few years ago, right after she finished college. The previous owner, Mrs. Catherine Woods had fallen ill with cancer and needed to sell her pride and joy. She felt Ava had the right spirit to run her specialty store and stayed on long enough to train her before she retired. What started out as a job 'to pay the bills before the career in marketing took off', soon became her passion too. Ava stayed on and eventually bought the business from the Woods family after Catherine passed away. Funny how we make plans for this and that, and the Lord steps in and redirects our paths.

Upon entering into the store she was immediately surrounded by the fragrant aroma of pumpkin spice and serenaded by Beethoven in the background. Although they were a year round Christmas store, she decided a year or so ago to honor the other seasons or holidays too with a small display when you first walked in the door. Halloween was just a few days away so the pumpkin display was front and center.

"Maggie, you are a godsend! Thank you so much for opening for me this morning." She said setting her pocketbook down behind the counter and taking another sip of her hot chocolate.

"Girl it was nothing, I was already up and dressed. How was Miles this morning?" She inquired, grinning from ear to ear.

"Mags, come on. You know Miles and I are *just* friends. We're a couple of business associates, helping one another out." She stated her case almost as if she was trying to convince herself of their status, and not her friend.

"Pffft. Ava, I know *you,* and I have seen how he looks at you. You two are the only ones that don't seem to realize what everyone else seems to know, and that is you're in love." To which Ava rolled her eyes.

The chiming of jingle bells signaled that they now had a customer, and gave a whole new meaning to the expression 'saved by the bell'.

Ava glided over to the middle aged woman perusing the snowman section. "Hi, may I help you find anything in particular?"

"I just love snowmen! You have a fantastic selection. I am actually doing a little pre-Christmas shopping recon." She said wide eyed and giggling.

Ava brushed her long curly blonde hair from her shoulder, and smiled graciously. "I completely understand. Feel free to look around and let me know if I can be of help. We also offer lay-away." The lady made a small clapping motion continuing to look at all the different figurines, and ornaments.

La Noel was a specialty store offering year round Christmas themed gifts, ornaments, and figurines made from a variety of materials such as wood, glass, metals and paper. Ava always sought out things that you could not get at the local box stores. She especially loved hand crafted and unusual imported pieces and boasted that her store had the best selection of nativity scenes, bar none.

Maggie came up alongside of Ava as she was rearranging an angel display, draping her arm around Ava's waist whispering, "So tell me what he was wearing today? Khakis and the dark red shirt? Or was he in jeans and the light blue shirt. I *love* that one! It brings out his eyes." She teased. Ava could not help but grin at her best friend, then proceeded to describe Miles from head to toe, getting lost in the day dream of him.

Maggie Willis had been her best friend for the better part of fifteen years. They met at a church camp event and instantly became inseparable. They lived only a few miles apart as it turned out and eventually went to the same high school. Maggie was taller than Ava and slender with short dark unruly natural curly hair, big brown eyes and a personality the size of Texas. She was witty, smart and hardworking. Aside from helping out at La Noel, she was a L.P.N. and worked closely with the youth at her church and at risk girls. Her pull no punches, say what's on your mind demeanor seemed to resonate with the younger women and they not only liked but respected her. She and Ava looked like Mutt and Jeff standing side by side. Ava was petite at five one with big blue eyes, long natural curly blonde hair with a fair complexion. Ava was gentle, unassuming and was always there when someone needed something. She had a gracious spirit and a laugh that would light up a room. They made a good team with each of them bringing their own strengths to the table.

Once again the jingle bells alerted them that customers were coming and going and it was time to get back to work. They were unusually busy for a Tuesday and the day seemed to go by quickly, for which Ava was grateful. Soon they were tallying up the daily tickets and getting the deposit ready for the bank.

"Wow that's a really decent day Avie. Twelve hundred, fifty five dollars and eighty four cents!"

"Seriously? I bet that porcelain angel, the one we got from Spain is what put us over. Mrs. Fowler has had her eye on that for months, I'm pleased she was able to get it."

"Hey, since you are headed over to the coffee shop do you want me to go ahead and drop the deposit off at the bank night drop?"

"Would you? That would really save me some time."

"For you my dear, of course!" she said with a toothy grin.

"Thanks Mags."

She finished the deposit while Ava finished vacuuming the store and then straightened the countertop. It was five after six when Maggie locked the front door behind Ava, and headed out the back door towards her car. It was a little cooler tonight than Ava expected and she quickly made her way into the shelter of the Café. She loved the way the Café made her feel. It exuded a warmth and friendliness that most of the chic trendy chains stores lacked, well that and the fact that the owner was extraordinarily handsome didn't hurt.

There were several people in line at the counter and few scattered around the Café sitting at tables with their heads buried in their smart phones and laptops. The aroma this evening was different than it was this morning, richer and robust with a hint of cinnamon. Katie was busy behind the counter, but appeared to have everything under control. She was the most experienced Barista Miles had and she was quite something to watch, her moves were quick, smooth, and fluid. She really should have been Miles's morning barista, but since she was going to school during the day he let her work at night.

Ava didn't see Miles right away so she secured a table in the corner near the window and sat facing the counter. Removing her scarf she laid it on top of her purse and set her phone on the table next to the binder that held her notes and clippings.

Miles came up behind her laying his large warm hands on her shoulders. She leaned back then looked up and was lost in the gaze of his green eyes. His smile revealed his dimples and her stomach turned flips as he swung into a chair next to her. His knee rested against hers as he scooted up to the table. He had Katie bring them both a bottled water.

"Did you change clothes?"

"Yes. A Barista in training accident. I got soaked." He said laughing.

"Oh No!"

"It's all good. I just ran home about an hour ago, took a quick shower and changed. Ok, I have to be honest, I'm at a total loss for a theme this year. I'm afraid I'm at your mercy once again."

"No worries I have a ton of ideas." She flashed him her confident reassuring grin.

Ava had decorated his Café for Christmas for the last three years, each time with a different theme. Each year she had managed to outdo what she had done the year before, and Miles was amazed at her ingenuity. He could already tell he was going to have a difficult time concentrating being in this close proximity to her. Leaning in he could smell the faint scent of her shampoo lingering in her hair, and inhaled deeply.

For the next hour or so they went over ideas for Café decorations as well as plans for the large live spruce he cut every year and placed in the far corner of the Café near the opposite window. Their conversation was light, spirited and filled with laughter. This was always the case with them. There was this underlying sexual tension between them but once they started talking it was if they were in their own bubble and there was just the two of them. They were comfortable and relaxed so the conversation just flowed.

After two hours, Miles leaned back in his chair to stretch and then muttered something under his breath she couldn't quite make out. A couple was entering the Café and Miles's relaxed demeanor changed to one of pensiveness. He put his hand over hers, and spoke softly, "Do you mind if we take a small break?"

In walked a man in a dark suit who suddenly appeared at their table with his date on his arm.

"Taking a break Miles?" His tone dripping with sarcasm. Miles stood.

"Sebastian, always a pleasure. Allow me to introduce my friend and fellow shop keeper, Ava Turner. Ava, this is my older brother Sebastian."

She started to stand with her hand out reached to shake his and he leaned in taking her hand then kissing the back of it. Visibly startled she nodded and sat back down in her seat then looked cautiously over at Miles.

"It's nice to meet finally you Sebastian. I've heard so much about you, it's hard to believe our paths have not crossed before now."

Sebastian smiled slyly and then introduced his date for the evening, a Claire something, she didn't quite catch her last name. Miles turned to Ava and excused himself for a moment then walked his brother and date over to the counter where Katie took their order. They stood chatting for a few moments then Miles came back to the table. He sat quietly and she wondered what was going through his mind, his mood had changed so quickly. She could see the resemblance between the two brothers, Miles was slightly taller but Sebastian was still a good six feet two inches himself. He was thinner than Miles and his hair was a little darker and cut short, but they had the same striking hazel green eyes. They both had strong jaw lines with dimples but Miles had a smaller nose and perfect bow shaped lips. Sebastian carried himself in a very confident smooth manner, and she thought to herself, he is probably one that rarely hears the word "no".

He and his date stopped by momentarily at the table again on their way out to say goodnight, since they were on their way to dinner. Once the door shut behind them, Miles let out an audible exhale. Taking that as her queue, "I've kept you too long, I'm sorry." She started to put her clippings away.

"No, I'm sorry. Please, let me buy you dinner. I'm starving, I know you've got to be hungry. Michael and Katie are closing up tonight." He flashed her a tentative smile, and put his hand over hers to stop her paper shuffling. Her shoulders dropped and as she looked into his eyes she saw the angst he was trying so hard to disguise. She paused then said "You know, I am starving now that I think about it. How about Mexican?"

"Perfect!" He grinned unleashing those magnificent dimples.

She waited inside the Café while he pulled around in front to pick her up. His late model Range Rover pulled curb side and she hurried out to meet him, he waited with her door open and helped her put her things away. Third Day was playing on the radio and he had the heater cranked up to keep her warm. She loved how thoughtful he was and knew he would make some lucky woman a great husband one day.

They drove about five miles to the Mexican restaurant at the edge of town, where a large birthday party was taking place. Even though the place was crowded they were seated right away and enjoyed the lively atmosphere and entertainment. It was hard to carry on a conversation with all the noise but they were managing, laughing and just enjoying themselves. It felt good to let go and be alone together. They finished eating dinner and then decided to share a sopapillia, the perfect end to a spicy meal. He drove her back to her car then waited until she was settled and watched her drive away.

Chapter 2

Family Tree

*M*iles circled back around to the front of the Café to make sure that Michael and Katie were ok, and they looked to still have about fifteen people inside the Café. Katie looked up from the counter and waived him off. He smiled and waved back. Then he headed out of town and down the highway that led to their estate. It wasn't that Miles was ashamed of his family's money, but he certainly wasn't one to flaunt it. That was not his nature.

At twenty six years old he still drove the same late model Land Rover he bought when he was seventeen, and was frugal with what money he did make. He felt blessed to have grown up with so much privilege, but with it came enormous responsibility. His family bought the eighty five acre estate when the boys were seven and ten, his mother wanted them in a place where they could run, roam and still be safe. They attended a private school in the city, but their home was their haven. At one time his family had shown horses, mostly Quarter horses, and boasted of a few champions in their time. They also had riding horses, another passion his mother instilled in him. The barn was fully staffed, and the people who were hired to care for the equines lived on the property in a lavish apartment above the barn. They had a son, Max, who was Miles's age and they became the best of friends.

After about ten years, his father got out of the show and stud business then sold most of the horses to a farm in Kentucky. Max's family went with the horses and all that remained at the barn were his mother's riding horse, and two others that the boys rode and took care of while they were home. Miles's mother came from a wealthy family that lived in Boston. She was a world class violinist and at the age of sixteen was studying at Julliard and playing part time with the Boston pops. At nineteen she met his father in New York at a Cathedral she was playing in and it was love at first sight.

His father, Thomas, who was eight years her senior, was a self-made man who worked hard, invested wisely and selected diverse business opportunities to put his capital towards. He was in New York on business when he stopped at the historic cathedral that lit up the corner of the city block, he was drawn by the music that had wafted outside to the street. Once inside he saw her on the alter playing the violin, and he thought to himself she was the most beautiful creature he had ever seen. He stayed and listened to the recital and then remained afterward in the sanctuary in hopes of meeting her. The pamphlet listed her name as Mary Elizabeth Barrow. Finally, she emerged and he introduced himself and invited her to dinner.

She accepted his invitation and that was thirty eight years ago, thankfully today they are still very much in love. She continued to travel and play all over the United States and Europe until she got pregnant with Sebastian. Once she had Miles she officially retired from the music business and only took assignments that would allow her to stay close to home to be with her boys. Theirs was a storybook love affair full of travel and romance. It was a relationship Miles hoped to emulate one day with his wife.

He pulled into the main gate and punched in his code. The gate swung open and Miles drove down the road that led past the stables, and the main house until he pulled into the small driveway at the guest cottage which was located beyond the garden and pool. This had been his humble abode for the past couple of years and he was content here. It afforded him the privacy he desired, but he was close enough to look in on his mom since his father and Sebastian still traveled internationally for weeks at a time. After finishing college he had come back home in hopes of finding a job in the business community, but the recession hit and jobs were scarce.

That is when his father purchased then renovated the old abandoned Murk's diner in downtown Mapleton and turned it into the Caffeine Infusion Café. He decided to let Miles run it while he was awaiting a real job opportunity to present itself, but the Café suited Miles and his personality. He loved developing relationships with fellow shop keepers, reaching out to the community and churches and inviting people in to his Café. He manage to create a warm friendly environment where everyone was welcome and were made to feel like family. With a lot of long hours and hard work Miles had not only created a comfortable little Café haven, he was also turning a profit and increasing his revenues annually.

Sebastian three years his senior had graduated college early and had worked for a large tax accounting firm, he traveled the world and audited large corporations. He had an apartment in the city about twenty five miles from the small town of Mapleton, where they currently lived. Sebastian on the other hand thought the Café beneath them and sneered at Miles's accomplishments considering them meager compared to his own. Miles however was proud of Sebastian with all that he had achieved in the few short years he had worked at the firm, and just recently began working with his father in the family business. Mr. Petersen believed it would be best if the boys worked for someone else first for a period of time, before they came to work for him. There were times Miles considered going back out into the work force and leaving the Café behind, since that is what his father expected of him.

Miles did not have that ruthless, win-at-all cost desire or conquer-the-world ambition and loathed the idea of giving up the Café and leaving behind the relationships he had established. He was proud of the work he was doing there and the service he provided despite what the men in his family thought. Miles's disposition was like that of his mother's. He was sensitive and creative with a servant's heart. He was active in his church and liked the benefits that a small town provided. Sebastian could have the bright lights and the big city life; he was content in Mapleton.

He gathered his duffel bag out of the back of the car and before he could shut the door he heard the panting and thunder of padded paw prints of Zelda, the family golden retriever. She heard him come in the gate and chased his car all the way back to the cottage.

"Hey girl! Miss me today?" Her tail furiously wagging back and forth answered his question. He bent down to rub her ears, kissed and patted the top of her head. She bounded inside the cottage behind him and circle around in front of the fireplace several times and then plopped down on her fluffy pillow. Her big brown eyes stared up at her beloved Miles. He took his cell phone out of his pocket and dialed a number.

"Hello, Miles?"

"Mom, yeah hi, I just got in. Just wanted to let you know I've got Zelda for the night."

"I figured, she was pacing like a cat on a hot tin roof waiting for you. I let her outside when I heard the gate alarm beep."

"Well that's one gal I can always count on to love me regardless…. Are you ok up there?"

"Yes, your father got home around seven tonight, which was a pleasant surprise."

"Ok, good! I love you Mom, have a good night."

"Sleep well my son. I love you."

Miles kicked off his shoes, and sat back on the couch relieving the events of the day. The thought of Ava made him smile and he didn't realize how tired he was until just now. Glancing over at the clock on the kitchen wall reminded him he had been up for over nineteen hours. He pulled himself off the couch and made his way into the bathroom to brush his teeth with Zelda right on his heels. Miles all but dove head first into the king-sized bed, covered with Egyptian cotton sheets and a down comforter that was soft, warm and luxurious. The sheets felt cool against his skin and he snuggled under the fluffy duvet. There was a quilt at the foot of the bed, and Zelda launched up there, claiming that as her own. Once her master was settled in bed, she laid her head across his feet. He fell asleep and dreamed of Ava.

Ava's ride home lasted all of three minutes. She lived downtown in her grandparent's house. Her grandfather passed when she was a baby, and her grandmother passed away a few years back. Her mother and Aunt Sybil insisted she take the house since she and her grandmother had been so close. They both had homes of their own and neither one had any intention of moving back into their childhood home again. Plus her cousin Adam had recently gotten married, and they had moved into the city to be near their jobs.

She had worked very hard over the last couple of years renovating the house to make the place her own. It was a two story traditional craftsman style home with a large front porch, and brick lower façade and taupe siding on the upper part. Her grandfather had been the foreman at the textile mill and built the home when Ava's mom was a toddler. It was a perfect home for a small family and they had been very happy there. Ava had painted the outside shutters a matte black and painted the front door a burgundy wine color complete with the welcoming wreath on the front door.

The inside was decorated in calm hues of sea foam green and pale yellows with a cottage style shabby chic theme. For the most part paint and new furniture were the extent of the inside renovations with the exception of the updated kitchen and master bathroom. Her cousin Adam was a builder who was instrumental in coordinating the kitchen and bath renovations. She could not have done it without his assistance. Her kitchen now boasted of new cabinetry, double ovens, gas stove and a large kitchen island with a sink. If the truth be told, her kitchen was worth more than the whole house put together. Since the house was paid for, and her plan was to stay there forever, the investment seemed well worth it. The house sat on a large corner lot at the intersection of Main Street and Park Avenue with the house actually facing Park Avenue. She had a large back yard that was fenced in with a decorative wooden privacy fence consistent with the town's historical preservation guidelines.

Large oak and maple trees adorned the back and side yards with a few flowering ornamental trees in the front yard. Pulling up in the driveway of this house always felt like home to her. The house itself was deceptively large on the inside. It had a huge great room with a large fireplace, a dining room that now opened up into the kitchen, and a large laundry-mud room and master bedroom with on suite bath on the lower level. Upstairs there was a large wide hallway with two large bedrooms, a spacious hall bathroom and a smaller room her grandmother used as a sewing room. She used it as an office.

She knew all of the neighbors that lived down her street and felt very safe there. After work during the summers, she would walk through town, up and down the residential streets and chat with people as she exercised. Most of the families had lived there for years, but more and more homes were being bought or passed down to people like Ava, and there seemed to be a rebirth of sorts happening in Mapleton. Just like the stores downtown were also experiencing a new influx of shops and restaurants drawing people back into town. What once was a small town on the decline with abandoned stores on every corner, was now a thriving community once again. Ava for one was proud to be a part of that revitalization effort.

She was pleased that she had made the decision to go to dinner with Miles. The whole interaction with his brother was a little intense, and she was relieved to see him relax again once they got to the restaurant. Ava was restless tonight with a lot on her mind. Besides Miles, who lately she seemed to be thinking of constantly, she was involved in trying to expand her storefront. Mr. Bateman who had the plumbing supply store that was located between her and the Caffeine Infusion Café, was closing his store. He had been in ill health lately and his son, had moved to Chicago years ago and so he was going to close and retire early. Big box stores had all but killed his business, but he was grateful for the faithful few builders who still traded with him, but it was not enough to keep the business going. She was hoping to pick up his lease and expand her store giving her more storage and a public restroom which she now currently lacked.

The property manager was accepting bids and proposals for that space for the next two weeks, then they were going to make a decision. Ava had gotten her personal and business financials together so now she needed to get with Adam on the proposed renovations. This would be a huge risk for her, expanding the business and the added overhead the new space would surely deliver. She also knew if God was calling her to take this chance and expand her business, He would provide. She stopped and sat on the couch for a moment, and prayed. She lifted up Miles and his brother, and she also prayed for guidance in this store expansion, and for wisdom. Ava felt calmer after spending time in prayer, after that she put her clippings away in her office and got ready for bed. Tomorrow was another day and she had a large order arriving so she needed to be at the store early to get ready for the shipment.

Chapter 3

Could this be love

Ava arrived at the store at seven a.m. then started consolidating and moving boxes around to make room for the new holiday shipment. Now even more the expansion into the neighboring store front was weighing on her mind, she could really use the extra space. Once she had completed all she could do in the store room she decided to head over to the Café and get a muffin and some hot chocolate. She locked the front door behind her and stopped briefly to peek in the windows of the plumbing supply store. His inventory was extremely low now, and the sign in the window stated there was a fifty percent sale on everything in the store, and *all sales were final*. FINAL. That word really jumped out at her this morning and she was suddenly very melancholy. She felt bad that he was in poor health, that he had no one to pass his life's work onto, that this was and end of an era for him and she felt bad that she wanted his space.

Ava walked into the Café now completely depressed. There was already a line of people trying to get their morning dose of caffeine before they got to the daily grind of their jobs. Miles spotted her immediately then walked over and put his hand to her back guiding her over to a small table. "Hey what's wrong? I could see when you walked in that you were upset."

"Oh Miles, I feel horrible. As you know, Mr. Bateman is closing his store, and I am planning to put in a bid for his space which I am desperately needing. I've been so worried about getting all my ducks in a row with financials and working on my renovation proposal that I haven't stopped to think about how this is impacting *him* and his life. I feel so selfish." She said tearing up.

"Hey don't cry." He said pulling a handkerchief out of his pocket.

"Thanks. Wow you don't see these very often anymore." She said with a sniffle. He smiled and laid his large warm hands over hers and stroked the back of her hand with his thumb.

"I know what you mean Ava, but honestly I think he's worked hard for so long and the last few years have been a struggle. I think he is ready for a change. I don't think he would begrudge either one of us if we wanted to expand into his space."

Miles was trying to console her however, her heart sank a little further with his last sentence. She had no idea that he also wanted the space to expand the Café. Honestly, there was no way she could compete with the Petersen's. Financially they could afford to buy the entire downtown block and then some. She managed a weak smile and dabbed at her eyes with the handkerchief.

"I had no idea you wanted to expand the Café, I guess that means we are sort of... competing for the space."

"Well it's more Sebastian than me really. I mean of course I can always think of ways to use the space, but I think the landlord wants to make sure the building goes to the right person for the right reasons. Our building is one of the largest, since we have the full basement, main floor and then the loft. I think Mr. Bateman's store has a partial basement and the main floor and yours has neither. So I think you stand a really good chance."

"I hope he's that honorable. I don't know, I've just had a lot on my mind lately so I guess I'm a little emotional."

"That's ok, I understand I really do." He stated sympathetically, his hands still on hers. She gazed into his beautiful eyes, and the gentle expression they held.

"Not to change the subject, but did you hear about the film crew that is coming through to scout out this area for a scene in the upcoming Brett Parker movie? Supposedly they are coming through here tomorrow or Friday." He stated trying to divert her attention and cheer her up.

"No I hadn't!" she exclaimed perking up a bit. "How exciting is that?"

"It could be a big boom for business if they select Mapleton to film part of the movie in. I hope they stop and go through downtown, I'm not sure where in the county they are going to be scouting, only that we were one of the top picks." Miles said unleashing that dazzling smile. Ava looked down at her watch and panicked when she realized it was nearly nine a.m.

"Oh Miles, I'm so sorry I have to go! I have a huge order coming in and well, he's probably there waiting on me now! I didn't realize how much time had passed by."

"You didn't even get your breakfast, you get going, and I'll bring something down for you in a few minutes."

"Miles, thank you so much!" She stuffed the handkerchief in her pocket as she scurried to get back to her store.

Ava had just unlocked the front door and turned the 'open' sign in the window, when she heard someone pounding on the back door. The timing was impeccable. She checked through the peep hole in the back door and it was the delivery man. Opening the door and swinging it wide, Ava tried to make room for him to get the hand truck through the store room to the area she had cleared off. The label on his shirt said SEAN and he appeared to be quite chipper for an early morning delivery. He wasted no time in unloading the truck and soon she had boxes literally from the floor to the ceiling.

He had her sign the delivery notice and was gone, the whole episode took ten minutes from start to finish. The actual unpacking and arranging of the items would take her days! Standing there surveying her new inventory she began feeling completely overwhelmed. The sound of jingle bells on the front door snapped her out of her moment of self-pity. Ava walked out from behind the curtain partition that separated the front counter from the store room and saw Miles grinning from ear to ear with a basket full of muffins with a coffee for Maggie and a hot chocolate for her.

He was pleased to do this for her, since it was usually Ava taking baskets of goodies or get well baskets to people in the community. That is one of the many things Miles loved about her. She would hear of someone in town who was sick or had lost a loved one, and she would set up a meal plan for them, or take them a basket that was full of thoughtful practical things. She would send handwritten notes and letters on stationery, and it was those personal touches that made her special to so many people.

"Miles! That is so sweet. Thank you! Maggie will be here any minute and I know she will be so grateful. She swung by the bank to get change for us."

They heard the back door slam and surmised that Maggie had arrived. They could hear her well before they ever saw her, "Oh ….My….Gosh. Ava! Guess what I heard at the bank today?" Then the curtain came slinging sideways and there she stood with a plastic sunflower clipped in her unruly hair, her bright blue knit sweater dress and large black buckled belt cinched her waist along with her cowboy boots. What an entrance.

"Oh have mercy! Hi Miles, I didn't know you were here. Holy cow Ava, what's with all the boxes girl? That is gonna take us a week to sort through. Miles I hope those muffins are for us and you're not just standing there teasing me with breakfast." She spoke in rapid fire style.

Miles and Ava both busted out laughing as Maggie walked over and reached for a banana nut muffin then the coffee. She stood on her tip toes, kissed Miles on the cheek, and then headed back to the office muttering to herself about all the boxes. Ava shook her head and giggled as she walked from around the register and Miles closed the gap between them and set the basket on the counter.

"Seriously Miles, that was very sweet of you to bring this down for us, let me pay for…" She started and he waved her off.

"No please it's on the house. You've had a rough start to your day, and I wanted to do something nice for you."

She leaned in and hugged him and he reciprocated drinking in her scent. They both lingered there for a minute or so, until Miles's phone started to ring. Reluctantly he released her then reached in his shirt pocket for his phone. It was Sebastian.

He looked at his phone and then down at her, "I'm sorry, I really ought to take this call. See you later?"

Smiling and with a nod "Of course. I'll come by after I close, we can walk to church together."

With that he answered the call, turning and walking outside where he eventually ended up sitting on a park bench in front of the Café.

"Do you have all that paperwork together that I asked you for on Monday?" Sebastian barked.

"Good Morning Sebastian. I'm great, thanks for asking. To answer your question, yes I have the majority of it together. I had a question about last quarter though."

"I told you the other day not to worry about last quarter's forecast, that I would have it completed by the time we submit. Do you have the sketch ready? It needs to be finished by Friday. This is really a no brainer for Mr. Anderson, but I want it all to look above board."

"What do you mean a no brainer? You can't be sure that no one else is going to bid on this Sebastian." Miles said exasperated.

"Miles do you know something I don't? If so, spill it. I'm ready to get this phase finished and behind me. It's not that skirt next door is it? Tell me she's not actually going to throw her hat in the ring, is she?"

"How dare you! I will not..." Miles was abruptly cut off by Sebastian when he had to take an "important" call.

Miles was furious, Sebastian could be so crass sometimes it was hard to believe that they had the same mother. He hadn't always been that way, perhaps the business world he now dealt with had turned him ruthless and hard. Either way this conversation was not over, and Miles was not going to be so easily dismissed. Not this time.

The Café was really busy this morning and Natasha, Tim and the new kid Sammy were getting a work out. By two o'clock in the afternoon things had slowed down, and Miles decided to head upstairs to the loft and work on the sketch for the bid. Ava's words kept floating in and out of his mind, and he could read between the lines. If it came down to just the two of them bidding on the space, more than likely the Petersen's would win. He knew it and apparently she knew it too. He stood and stretched, then paced. It was times like this he wished his family's money was not an issue and it was an 'all things created equal' situation.

He started working back on the sketch, he put his finishing touches on it when he had a brilliant idea. He quickly began sketching a second version. His original one with the large group/party room theme for the Café, and one with a split theme that had him taking half the space and Ava the other half. When he next looked down at his phone, he saw that he had missed a text and it was five thirty. The text was from Nick Reardon, the youth pastor at his church, begging him to take the youth group tonight because he was sick.

He put the sketches in the portfolio and locked it in his office. Grabbing his bible Miles came down stairs with a lightness he had not felt since seeing Ava this morning. He loved the idea of a compromise on the building space, and he couldn't wait to share his idea with her. The shift change at the Café had already taken place and Katie and Michael were there already working the crowd of post work regulars.

"Hi guys." Miles said as he placed his hand on Katie's shoulder. She smiled and went back to the grinder for the espresso she was creating.

"Hey Miles," Michael stuck out his hand for a shake. "How's it going buddy?"

"Decent, really decent." Miles said with a smile. "I'm on my way to church, the youth leader has a stomach bug so I'm subbing tonight. Thirty five teenagers, wish me luck."

"LUCK!" They both yelled in unison as he walked out the door.

Miles laughed and shook his head as he headed across the street with his bible in hand then walked down a few blocks to Mapleton Baptist Church. His family was Protestant and he was raised in a Presbyterian church they attended in the city. He attended regularly until he met Pastor Mark Wilson a couple of years ago, and they became good friends. Mark was slightly older than Miles, but not by much and was one of the first regulars at the Café. Soon he and Miles were having long philosophical discussions on religion, the bible and God. Mark invited him to attend a special service they were having one Wednesday night, and after that Miles was hooked. He had never heard the word presented quite that way, it was challenging and his message was so thought provoking. Mark had a way of explaining the word that was true, informative and humorous and his appeal spanned generations. Miles gave his life to Christ that Wednesday night.

Soon after, he was attending a men's Sunday school class and was assisting the youth pastor when he could. For the first time in his life, the word seemed real, and he was truly learning what it was like to have a relationship with the one true living God. There was nothing else like it and the Lord had become a priority in his life. It didn't hurt that after a couple weeks of attending services that he realized Ava also attended that church and had been sitting four rows behind him the whole time. Serendipity. That is how Miles liked to refer to that little coincidence.

He entered the sanctuary stopping momentarily to speak to a couple of the parishioners and waved at Mark in the pulpit as he made his way back to the youth meeting room. Turns out the bug had made its way through the local high school and the group was down to about seventeen tonight. They took prayer requests, chatted about what was going on at school and then continued on through the book of John, chapter two. Time passed so quickly and before they really got started with the discussion, it was time to dismiss.

"Jake would you close us in prayer tonight?" Miles requested. Soon the young man began praying, Miles was so impressed with Jake's spiritual maturity and reflected on where he was at that age in his walk with God. Jake definitely had a head start on him and he was proud of the man Jake was becoming. Miles thought *thankfully our walks with God are not a competition or a race, they are a marathon full of ups and downs with spiritual challenges. God is with us, and if we seek him, He guides us the whole way. God please direct me and give me wisdom with Sebastian….and with Ava.*

The kids dispersed, leaving Miles behind to straighten chairs and put away the study guides. He was almost finished when he heard, "So. You stood me up!" There stood Ava with her hands on her hips and a determined look on her face.

"Oh No! Ava I'm so sorry! I did. I totally did. Sebastian had me working on something for him and I lost all track of time. Then Nick texted me that he was sick, and could I take the youth tonight, and well yeah, I totally forgot." He hung his head in mock shame and his brown wavy locks fell into his eyes and framed his handsome face.

"Oh it's ok, I see how I rate on your scale. Mm hmm." Still feigning anger, she cracked as soon as he looked up through those wisps of hair and gazed over at her with his beautiful green eyes.

"Puppy dog eyes!! Really Miles? No fair!" She exclaimed. They both grinned. She helped him with the last of the chairs and they turned off the lights and headed back towards the sanctuary.

They were lost in conversation when Mindy Lewis came rushing over interrupting them, completely oblivious to the fact that they were having a private moment. She got right in between Ava and Miles, pulling on his arm to drag him over to a pew.

"Oh, hi Miles, I was hoping to catch you, I just have to talk to you about our ladies group meeting that we are having over at the Café. It's for our quarterly meeting that's next week. I need to check on the space and pricing and well everything. Here have a seat and I'll get my pad out, I have a ton of questions." She prattled on and did not draw breath until he was sitting in front of her sporting a deer in the head lights look. It was not in Miles's nature to be rude, plus he was caught a little off guard in the frantic way in which she ambushed him, so he sat.

Ava could see he was going to be a while and so she gracefully backed up and motioned for him to text her later. He gave her the sincere 'I'm sorry face' as he attempted to follow Mindy and the frenetic pace at which she spoke. Ava actually felt sorry for him. Because he was such a great guy, it caused all the single ladies at church to plot and plan ways to try and bump into him to get his attention. Miles was so gracious and kind that most of them never realized that he was rejecting their advances. As a matter of fact most of the people at church with the exception of the college girls and single moms, thought Miles and Ava were already a couple. They always sat together during services, and were often seen having lunch or dinner out together through the week, so people just came to their own conclusions.

Ava drove the short distance home and headed straight for the kitchen, she was starved. She and Maggie were grateful Miles had brought them breakfast, since they ended up working straight through lunch. Between customers and working in the store room, taking inventory and rearranging merchandise for the upcoming holiday season they had lost all track of time. Ava made herself a salad and reheated a cup of soup. It wasn't really what she was hungry for, but for now it hit the spot. She sat on the couch then turned on the television and surfed through the eighty five channels of 'nothing interesting'. Finally she settled on the Food Network, if she wasn't going to eat something fabulous and life changing, she could watch someone cook it.

A little before ten her phone rang, and it was Miles. It rang twice before she answered.

"Hello?"

"Ava? Hi it's Miles."

"Are you just now getting home from church?"

"Sort of. I left the church about eight fifteen and then ran by the Café to pick up something I left in my office. I got sidetracked talking to a couple of customers and so I just ran through a fast food drive thru and well, finally now I am home. I'm sorry about today, I was hoping we could have gotten a sandwich at Ollie's."

"Oh Miles its fine. Really. Honestly I'm surprised you got away from Mindy before nine." She said laughing.

"Tell me about it, she's a nice gal, but she talks ninety miles an hour and jumps around so much it's hard to track with her. Seriously, I'm mentally exhausted." He said with a chuckle.

"Well finish telling me about the film crew. Did you hear any more about them? Maggie heard the same thing at the bank this morning too."

"No not really, not any more than we knew last night, Sebastian was telling mother and me about it. He knows the finance guy that funds the majority of the Brett Parker movies, and he called to say he was going to be in the area so he asked Sebastian to lunch. Apparently they knew each other in college."

"He runs with quite the crowd doesn't he? You guys are such opposites, aren't you?"

"I guess, there was a time when we were a lot alike. He's always been more competitive than me, and at times that has driven a wedge between us. Our parents strove to make sure we were both supported in our sports or art or music, whatever we pursued. Things are a little tense between us now because I want full control of the Café, and even though Sebastian doesn't want the Café, it's like he doesn't want me to have it either."

"I'm sorry to hear that Miles, I guess that's what I witnessed last night…. I could tell just his presence alone was stressing you out."

"Yeah, I shouldn't let him upset me. I know he does it partly because he *knows* he's getting to me. So juvenile really, usually I just ignore him. OK, I'm changing the subject…. So when are you going to invite me over to see the new kitchen? It's finished isn't it?"

"Yes! I *need* to do that. I totally love it, my cousin Adam did a terrific job. Now I just need to brush up on my cooking, I've been lazy and eating out too much lately. What's your favorite meal? I'll make it and have you over. I've been watching the Food Network lately and I'm feeling a little heady." She said laughing at herself.

"Don't tease me. I'm really a traditionalist when it comes to food. No caviar, swordfish and sprouts for this guy. Well, I say you can't go wrong with pot roast, carrots and potatoes." He said laughing.

"Oh that does sound good, especially with the weather turning cooler. Ok, I will make dinner for us, what night is good for you?"

"How about one night next week? Maybe Thursday? My family has company coming in for the weekend, and so they've committed me with various events for the duration of the visit. Don't get me wrong I love these people, they are truly like family to us, but they have pretty much planned my entire weekend for me. Usually I get a little bit of say about what goes on in my life, but this time it's different." He said with a chuckle.

"Bless your heart. That actually will work out well, I am in full inventory mode at the store and will most likely work late on Saturday, then that night give out candy for Halloween. Then there's church on Sunday, so that will give me time to shop and prepare. Oh wait…I have a trade show next week. How about the next Thursday?"

"That will work, it's a date. Well it's after eleven now, I need to let you go." He said, his voice reluctant, and they spoke for another thirty minutes.

"Man this day has been a blur, it's gone by so fast. Sleep well Miles, I'll see you tomorrow, ok?" Her voice sounding sleepy.

"Count on it. Good night."

"Night." She pressed the end button on her phone.

Oh my goodness! She thought, now fully awake. *Miles Petersen in my house! I better get busy, I want everything perfect.* If she was truly honest with herself, she would have to admit that she is crazy about Miles and has been for months. They started off with a great friendship which she cherished, but as of late he was constantly on her mind, and she longed to see him and be with him. Her mind often drifting to the way his perfect bow shaped lips move when he spoke. Why she had not made a move before now to share her feelings with him was beyond her. She jumped up from the couch, took her plate into the kitchen, rinsed it and put it in the dishwasher. She opened the refrigerator to see if she had any of the ingredients to make dinner. *Carrots. That was it? Great....* She reached into the drawer then started making her list for the grocery store. After it was completed, she stuck it under a magnet on the refrigerator door and headed off to bed.

She glanced at the clock on the nightstand and it was midnight. Six a.m. was going to come early tomorrow, even still in the late hours she laid in bed as her mind drifted off to thoughts of Miles. His strong muscular body, the woodsy clean scent of his cologne, and his smile, dimples, eyes, hands...the list went on. It wasn't just his physical looks, he was truly a great guy. Honest, sincere and funny, plus he loved the Lord. She felt safe with Miles physically and emotionally. He was the epitome of the total package. If he had a fault she hadn't found it yet, and that was fine with her.

Miles laid on the couch and reflected on their conversation and was excited she had invited him over for dinner. She had told him all about the renovations while she was going through it, and it sounded really nice. *What am I waiting on? Seriously? Every other woman I meet pales in comparison to her, I love being with her, near her. I'm miserable when I don't get to see her. I'm definitely ready to take our relationship to the next level. I need to take it to the next level. I am going to take it to the next level,* he determined and soon he drifted off, sleeping on the couch all night.

CHAPTER 4

The Box

The Café was abuzz with the possibility of Hollywood elites stopping by for a cappuccino or iced coffee. Even Katie came into work early, just in case. Apparently word had gotten out around town as well, so there were lots of people just milling around Main Street this morning and the traffic coming in was much heavier than usual. Miles was already running late, he over slept, spun through the shower, threw on clothes and did not take time to shave. He parked in front of the Café, trotted in, grabbed an apron and tied it around his waist. He started clearing tables and chatting up the customers who were in line and sitting around the Café. He was a natural with people, he could talk to just about anyone about anything.

Not to be outdone, Sebastian came sauntering in with his friend and a large part of the movie crew. There were probably fourteen people in the entourage, the director of photography, a couple were set directors, prop guys and one from wardrobe. Miles was now behind the counter manning the cash register. Sebastian made the introductions, and amazingly got the Café staff names correct. He was actually quite affable today like the old Sebastian used to be, and Miles missed that version of his brother.

One of the prop guys was actually a woman. An extremely tall, leggy blonde that looked more like a fashion model than a prop mistress. She was extremely tanned, wore a short skirt, UGG boots and a layered V-neck sweater. She zeroed in on Miles and was doing her best to charm him with her womanly wiles. Miles was certainly flattered by her attention and was being a little flirty himself. He was in the middle of telling her a funny story when he glanced down the line, and saw Ava expressionlessly staring at him. Miles quickly finished his story and told her it was nice to meet her and she offered her hand in a weak delicate hand shake. Taking one last look at Miles as she walked away to join her group, she waved, batted her lashes and flashed a perfect orthodontia smile.

He smiled weakly and waved back then quickly dropped his head down. Ava had made her way through the line and now stood in front of a wickedly handsome Miles sporting a five o'clock shadow and wind tossed hair.

"Hi." he said sheepishly, while wiping his hands on his apron.

"She's not the one for you ya know? It would *never* work out." She said very matter of fact.

"Oh? So who *is* the one for me?" he teasingly inquired, but secretly hoped she meant herself.

"I don't know. All I know is it should be someone... *shorter*." With that she slapped down two dollar bills on the counter, then turned and walked back to the La Noel grinning. He also smiled and shook his head as he watched her walk away, *I think I'm in love*.

She tagged Maggie in to go and get her coffee and hobnob with the faux celebrities. Maggie all but sprinted to the Café and nearly ran over Sebastian as they both tried to go through the door at the same time. He of course stepped back then apologized for his haste, and she introduced herself shaking his hand emphatically. He nodded, smiled politely and continued out the door. Sebastian stood outside talking to his former college mate and they arranged to meet for lunch in a couple of hours. The crew needed to scout out a few more places in the county and take some photos while the day light was decent.

Maggie marched up to the counter where she and Natasha high fived each other. "Girl tell me all the scoop!" Maggie said with a sly grin.

"Honey all I know is that Ava busted Miles flirting up a storm with the blonde prop mistress!" Natasha whispered loud enough for Miles to overhear.

"You are kidding me!" Maggie said stunned.

"It wasn't like that, come on Natasha. Maggie, it wasn't like that….." Miles tried to defend himself, but ended up walking away seeing their eyes rolling and their heads bobbing. The girls busted out laughing at him and then went on chatting about the morning's activities. He walked away and retreated into the safety of his office. He went back over the proposal for the office space then looked back over the drawings again. He planned to go over them with Sebastian tonight when they were both home for dinner. The Weston's were coming into town and mother had a nice dinner planned, hopefully they would get a chance to discuss it before the guests arrived.

Maggie walked back to the shop and found Ava covered up with customers. She made haste getting back in there and working the register. "I'm so sorry, it was dead when I was in here earlier by myself."

"It's ok. I think they all left the Café and came straight here!"

They finished taking care of the rush and sat down for a few minutes. "Ava, our man Miles was looking especially

f-i-n-e today."

"Oh, I hadn't noticed." She stated cutting her eyes over to Maggie with a sly grin.

"He was rocking the royal blue button down shirt, jeans and boots. Oh and the five o'clock shadow was a nice touch. I think if you weren't my best friend, I would have mauled him right there on the spot."

"You are awful Maggie!"

"Actually he's too nice for me… I think Sebastian is more my speed." She said laughing.

"You can't mean that!" Ava's mouth dropped open.

"I'm teasing Ava, but Sebastian is a challenge I think I could handle. He is nice looking, smart and wealthy. He just needs an attitude adjustment. Don't worry he doesn't scare or intimidate me." She said grinning.

"Oh dear Lord no! I don't think my nerves could take it. Girl you are crazy." Ava said laughing.

The rest of the day was fairly event free, so Maggie left a little early to meet with some of the girls from church for a bible study. Ava stayed a little longer and decided to rearrange the store closet again and move some things into the attic. They literally did not have room to turn around back there. More than likely she was going to have to do what she did last year, and store many of the empty boxes at her house. Thankfully she lived close. It was not very convenient, but necessary.

She thought she heard someone tapping on the front glass window and peeked through the curtains to see who it might be, and it was Miles. *Perfect! I could use a tall handsome man about now.*

"Ava?" He shouted through the glass. He saw the curtain flutter and then she appeared.

"Hi!" she said unlocking the door. "This is a surprise."

"I was getting ready to leave and I saw your car was still in the lot. It's dark so I just wanted to make sure you were ok."

"Thank you Miles, you are always so thoughtful. I'm still here trying to rearrange the eight thousand boxes I have in my mini-store room." She said waving her arms towards the back storage area.

Miles followed her back there, and saw the hundreds of boxes, all shapes and sizes that she was referring to. She did need the space he thought to himself.

"Say do you have a couple of minutes? I could really use your help."

"Absolutely, what do you need?"

"Well right now I need your height and long arms" she said laughing.

"Oh really? Do tell." He said unleashing a devilish grin exposing his dimples.

"Ok, in the attic is a large, but not heavy box. Just awkward. It's gotten kind of pushed back and I can't reach it from the ladder. Here's the thing, there are boxes on either side of it that are filled with glass and crystal items that are very fragile and breakable. If you can help me pull down the attic stairs and we can walk up there together I can show you which box I need, then I'll come down and once you grab the box, you can hand it down to me."

"Ok, I think I've got it."

He reached up and grabbed the cord that pulled the folding attic stairs down. Ava started up the stairs and got near the entrance of the attic and paused. Miles stepped up a couple of steps and was nearly as tall as Ava. Once he got in position he looked over at her and put his right hand in the small of her back to stabilize her. Feeling his hand on her back she turned and looked right into his eyes. They both felt incredibly drawn to one another, leaning into him slightly she felt Miles's mouth come gently down on hers.

His lips were warm and firm and he kissed her slowly at first, and immediately she reciprocated. With eyes closed, they were soon lost in one another, the kiss was long and sensual nearly taking her breath away. They parted only for a moment to catch their breath then came back together again, this time starting slowly and then progressing into something more passionate. Miles's left hand moved to cradle Ava's face, still holding her firmly at the back and he once again questioned *why had he waited so long to kiss her?*

The kiss seemed to go on forever, but she was not complaining. Ava had her hand resting on his chest and could feel the rhythm of his heartbeat through his shirt. She had never felt this way about anyone, not even the man she was previously engaged to marry. If this moment wasn't a testimony to the fact she made the right decision to walk away from that relationship, she didn't know what would be.

He gently pulled away then lightly kissed her nose, her cheeks and her lips once again. Nearly melting into his chest, Ava was praying that this moment would not end. Slowly she opened her eyes, and once again was looking into his beautiful green eyes with his long black eye lashes. He gazed into her vast blue eyes and was over taken with emotion, he knew right then and right there, *this* woman would have to be his wife. He was so in love with her and hope she felt the same way.

She was completely mesmerized by him, and realized now how much she truly loved and cared for him. Why had she been in such denial? Was she afraid of making the same mistake that she had made with Keith? Wasting two years of her life on broken promises, falling for his lies so he could manipulate her. She knew in her heart of hearts Miles was nothing like Keith. He had already proven that to her over the last couple of years, just in their friendship that he was worthy.

They stood there clinging to one another, neither willing to make the first move to break the bond they had just established. She could feel the hotness of his breath near her face, she leaned in closer and laid her head on his chest and he held her in his arms. The sound of his heartbeat was soothing and she wished that they were somewhere other than on the steps of the ladder to the attic.

"Hey baby, why don't you show me what you want me to retrieve, so I can get you down off this ladder? I know you can't be comfortable." He whispered to her. She lifted her head and kissed him lightly on the lips, then took another step up toward the opening. He came along side of her, moving his hand back to her waist to steady her once again.

"It's the tall white box with the red lettering. The brown boxes on either side hold the fragile stuff. This is fragile too so please be careful." She said softly.

He held her hand as she made her way to the bottom of the steps and then he climbed into the attic space and easily reached the fragile box. He turned to hand it down to her then made his way back down the steps. Then he folded the stairs back up and let the attic door shut. He wiped his hands on his jeans then walked over to where she stood.

"You ok?" he asked quietly, touching her cheek and delicately brushing a strand of hair out of her face.

"Yeah..." her voice just a whisper.

He took her hand and led her over to the small overstuffed love seat in her office. The one Maggie referred to as the 'fainting sofa' like ladies used to have during the 1800's. He laid back on it and brought her down on top of him. He wanted to feel her pressed up against him and hold her for just a bit longer. She willingly obliged. He was so tall and she was so petite that she filled in all the right grooves and he folded his long strong arms around Ava embracing her. He felt so right and she wished she could make up for all the lost time. After several minutes of just lying together quietly, he leaned up and began kissing her once again.

He knew he had to guard himself or they would never leave this back room. For this moment, he wanted little more than to continue kissing her, and keep sharing the intimate connection they had made.

She felt giddy as though she were back in high school and was being kissed by the dreamy senior she had always pined for. However, she was a grown woman, and he was a grown man and the passionate feelings they felt for one another were real. How would she ever walk back into the Café and not just fling herself at his feet? *Good Lord Ava, have some self-control!*

Ava felt something vibrating under her and she lifted up breaking their connection. Miles looked down and rolled his eyes, once again interrupted by his phone. It was Katie from the Café and she never called, which alarmed him.

"I'm so sorry, let me take this real quick." He sat up and answered. Katie apologized for interrupting his evening but several drunk people had come in and were giving them a bad time. Michael was there but was no match for a drunk crowd, however Miles, an athletic six three, two hundred pounds was not to be messed with. She sounded scared which was not like her and that really bothered him. He told Katie he would be right there.

Ava sensed from his side of the conversation that something was very wrong. He looked back at her and gave a reassuring smile, then quickly kissed her one last time.

"I have to go, they are in trouble. A bunch of drunks are giving them a hard time."

"Oh Miles. Then go! Don't worry about me, I'm fine. I'll see you tomorrow. Right?" As she waved him on.

"Yes of course, and hey you are right, you do need the space next door. This is crazy crowded." He looked back longingly at her and then quickly made his way out the backdoor sprinting to the Café.

Ava flopped back onto the sofa and wrapped her arms around her mid-section, a poor substitution for his strong muscular arms. She sat there quietly reliving every moment that they had shared together tonight. Now that it was truly out in the open she was elated and felt like she was floating. *Good luck getting to sleep tonight. That ship has sailed.* Finally she pulled herself up gathered her things and got ready to go home. She had no idea it was nearly ten o'clock.

She was worried about Miles and what he might be walking in to at the Café. He would never back down from a fight if he were protecting people he cared about, but he would also never start a fight. Usually just his size alone was off putting enough to make most people re-evaluate their decision to pick a fight with him.

She locked the back door and headed for her SUV. The short ride home was a blur, she must have been on auto pilot, not even remembering making turns or how she ended up in her driveway. Usually she would find that whole episode a little disconcerting if she were not so blissfully happy. She entered the house, and headed straight for bed, she didn't even want to eat supper. She just wished Miles would call and let her know everything was alright.

Miles entered the Café through the back door and came up slowly behind the counter. He could hear the man slurring his words and complaining loudly about his latte. Katie was trying to placate him and Michael was standing firm at the counter near the register. There were four of them and they had already run the other patrons who were in the Café out fairly quickly.

Miles stepped up with his deep baritone voice booming and announced that this was the last call and the Café was closing. The drunk man took one look at Miles and stepped back from the counter where he had been banging his fists. Miles towered over his stocky five foot eight inch frame, and quickly surmised that the alcohol definitely wiped away any inhibitions he might have had.

"Not only will you pay for the products that you wasted, you will apologize to her for being so rude."

"Who do you think you are, Mack?" He stated so slurred that Miles had trouble making it out.

Miles looked over to his friends who were not thinking this was as funny as it was earlier.

"I suggest you get your buddy and take him out of here *now*." He stated in a low deadly calm voice. "Or this is going to turn out really ugly for the four of you, and I don't think you want any of that."

One of the guys stepped forward and slapped a twenty dollar bill on the counter, called his drunk friend over and they grabbed his arms then walked him out of the Café.

Once they were gone, Miles locked the door, turned and walked back to the bar. Katie was standing there doing her best to hold it all together, and when Miles came around the corner, she threw herself at him bursting into sobs. He hugged her patting her on the back letting her release all her tears.

She pulled herself together and wiped her eyes, "I'm so sorry Miles. He was being so vulgar and kept slinging stuff around and it just frightened me. Michael tried to step in and then all four of them ganged up. I didn't know if they were just being jerks or if they were going to rob us or hurt us…." Her voice choked up again.

"Hey guys, listen it's not a problem. I am so sorry you were exposed to that. Michael, are you ok buddy?"

"Yeah I'm just really pissed off right now." He said embarrassed with adrenaline flowing, his voice wavering as he tried to busy himself counting the cash drawer.

"Ok, Michael, why don't you get the till, and Katie why don't you go sit in my office until we are ready to leave, I'll get this mess cleaned up and we'll walk out together." His voice sounding calm and in control.

They quickly tidied up and Michael wrote up the deposit and after about fifteen minutes, they were ready to go. He would text Natasha and let her know that the Café would not be set for them in the morning, and apologize. This happened rarely and for that Miles was grateful. This was maybe the third time in five years that he has had to handle drunk patrons. The first group was just loud and silly, but the last two groups were more aggressive.

Miles walked them over to Michael's car since he offered to take Katie to her house. Although Katie was feeling much better now, Michael said he would feel more comfortable if he could see her home. He would bring her back to her car in the morning. Miles waited until they had pulled onto the main street, then he got in his vehicle and headed out of the parking area. He stopped and decided to ride past Ava's house to check on her. He drove by slowly but didn't see any lights on so he kept on going and made his way to the highway that led him home. Probably for the best, if he had gotten to see her again, he would not have left willingly.

What a night! He finally got to kiss Ava, which was heavenly, then the near altercation at the Café, and then he also realized he missed his opportunity to speak with Sebastian about the bid for the space. His emotions were all over the map right now and he was feeling edgy.

He was pulling into the driveway, when his phone started vibrating, and he saw he had received a text from Ava. Quickly he grabbed the phone and read her text.

Miles, just laying here thinking of you and wondering if everything is alright? I know it's late, but let me know if everybody is ok. Prayed for you. ~Ava

He quickly texted her back.

Thanks for the prayers, situation under control, just pulled up to the house. Missing you. Sleep well, and I'll see you tomorrow.-Miles

Miles entered the cottage and headed straight for the bathroom and turned on the shower. While it heated up, he brushed his teeth, undressed and then stepped into the steamy hot shower. He stood leaning forward against the wall and let the hot water wash over him. His adrenaline had gotten into *fight or flight* mode at the thought of some punks harassing his employees. He was coming down off of that now and felt wiped out, he had been through a rollercoaster of emotions tonight and was ready to relax. After spending such sweet time with Ava, he now felt hollow without her, and somewhere deep inside him ached.

Ava laid awake staring at the ceiling thinking of Miles and wished she could hear his voice just once more tonight. She closed her eyes, and began praying, so many people with requests came rushing to her mind, and she was thankful that she had the privilege of praying for others. She finished and finally was starting to feel sleepy, when her phone started ringing. Ava rolled over and nearly knocked the phone off the night stand trying to answer it.

"Hello?" she said sleepily.

"Hi baby, I just had to hear your voice once more before I went to bed. I'm sorry if I woke you." his voice husky.

"No I'm lying here staring at the ceiling thinking of you, wishing you were here."

"Me too, I drove by your house when I left the Café....but I thought it best not to try and come in. You might never get rid of me."

"I could get used to you being around full time." She said wistfully.

"Get some sleep my love."

"You too, I can't wait to see you tomorrow."

She hung up the phone smiling, *Get some sleep my love! He does love me,* and finally fell asleep. Tomorrow could not come soon enough for her and she longed to be back in his arms.

Chapter 5

Candy

Miles was awakened by the pounding of fists on his front door. He stumbled out of bed and walked over to the door and looked out. Sebastian and his father were standing outside, and he wondered who had died. He unlocked the door and let them in, walked back to the kitchen then started making a pot of coffee. He looked over at the clock on the stove and saw it was 6:05a.m. *To what do I owe this honor?*

"Miles I see you've over slept again, is this becoming a habit?" Sebastian asked malevolently as he entered the kitchen.

"Sebastian." His father said coolly and gave him the look.

"Good morning Miles. Son, I have a request, and I'm acknowledging up front I know it will be inconvenient..." His father started.

Miles turned around to look at them both not sure of what was going to be said next. Sebastian looked bored, and his father took a seat at the table trying to look relaxed, but was visibly uncomfortable. Miles ran his hands through his hair trying to get it out of his face, and then took some coffee cups down out of the cupboards.

"Dad, what's going on?"

"As you know the Weston's arrived last night, and I understand you got in quite late."

"There was an incident at the Café and I ended up staying to close. I wanted to make sure everyone got off ok. I'm sorry I missed mother's dinner."

"That's fine, I hope everything is alright. Your mother of course was very concerned since no one had heard from you beforehand." Miles could hear the disappointment in his father's voice. Nothing angered his father more than to think his wife was upset, or hurt by someone else's thoughtlessness. A lesson the boys learned at a very early age.

"I will of course go up and speak to mother personally and apologize."

"That would be appreciated. Miles I have a favor to ask. The Weston's arrived from Washington last night, Bart was there on business, and Melissa accompanied him. Apparently Candace has wrecked her car and needs a ride here, which is where you come in son. We need for you to drive down to Atlanta and pick her up."

"Father, of course, I will do whatever is needed, but why doesn't she just rent a car and drive up?"

"I am really not at liberty to disclose that at this time. I need for you to please do this for us."

"Ok. When do I need to leave to get her and is she expecting me?"

"Now. Her father will call her and let her know." With that his father stood and slid the chair back under the table.

"What about the Café?"

"Sebastian will cover that today, since he has some business to attend to downtown."

"O-kay."

Miles walked them to the door and locked it behind them. He stood there leaning up against the door bewildered by what had just taken place. Atlanta was at least a five hour ride down depending on traffic, and he had little doubt that they expected him to pick her up curb side and turn right back around to bring her back without a break.

He fixed a quick cup of coffee, found his phone and texted Natasha to give her a heads up. She said it was slow thus far, so she was cleaning and setting up for the morning rush. He made his way into the bathroom, started shaving and getting ready to head up to the main house.

He walked down the driveway, cut through the garden and came in the back door to the main house. His mother and Melissa Weston were sitting at the breakfast bar having coffee and some fruit. He came in behind his mother and kissed her on the neck.

"Oh Miles!" She exclaimed giggling. "You startled me."

"I'm sorry mother, hi Aunt Melissa." He said dazzling them with his beautiful smile. "Mother, I want to apologize for last night, which was very inconsiderate of me not to call when I knew I was going to be delayed, and then ultimately absent."

"That's ok my son. I know it must have been important, since that was so out of character for you. I was worried though." He walked over and gave her a big hug and lingered there for a moment. "I'm so sorry you were worried. I feel even worse now. At first it started out as something unexpected that initially delayed me, but then some aggressive drunk patrons came into the Café and were giving Katie and Michael a hard time. There was really no time to think, I just reacted."

"Oh dear! Are you ok?"

"Thankfully he was no match for me in stature or condition and they ended up leaving peacefully, but my staff was pretty shaken up."

"Oh love, I'm so sorry. Please be careful. I could not bear it if something happened to you." she said emotionally.

Sebastian walked in and heard the last part of what his mother said. He looked pained for a moment then quickly recovered. He tossed his father's car keys at Miles, and remarked that it was gassed up and ready to go then laid the address down on the counter as to where he could pick up his charge.

"Sebastian, come here please. I need a hug from you as well this morning. I'm feeling a bit emotional after hearing Miles's story." His mother requested. He obliged her and drank in her fragrance then he wrapped his arms around her and nuzzled her neck. She hugged him tightly and held him for a minute. She didn't get this privilege often any more now that he was an adult. His mother had a way of calming him deep down in his soul. Sebastian knew in his heart that she loved him as much as she did Miles, but sometimes his head got in the way and jealousy crept in.

"I love you mom." He said softly in her ear.

"And I you." She said kissing his cheek.

"Where are my hugs and kisses from these strapping handsome young men??? What am I chopped liver?" Melissa interjected with mock indignation. Then both Miles and Sebastian turned and lavished their attention on Aunty Melissa which had everyone laughing, including Sebastian.

"I need to hit the road, and mother, I am truly sorry about last night." He hugged her one last time and headed for the garage to pick up his father's car, a black 2013 Mercedes S550. He got in and adjusted the seat then programmed the address into the G.P.S. If he had to take an unwanted road trip, this would be the car to take it in. The luxury vehicle was a dream to drive and he put his aviator sunglasses on and slung into the low rise leather seat. The seat was still warm from where Sebastian had taken the car and gassed it up. He turned on the satellite radio and found a classic rock station to get him started on this mystery journey he had been enlisted for.

It was still early and he hesitated to call Ava since she had gotten to bed so late last night. He needed to focus and get down to Atlanta and get back so he could see her. He settled into the fine leather seats and reminisced about last night as he made his way down the highway.

Ava felt especially rested even though she had only gotten about four hours of sleep. She labored over what she would wear today, she had styled her hair three different ways so far and still wasn't happy. She looked in the mirror and just stared at herself. Her big blue eyes returned the stare. It was cool this morning and wearing her hair down seemed to make the most sense. Therefore, the brown pants suit with the dark yellow mock turtleneck, with silver accessories would do for her attire today.

She made toast and juice her breakfast this morning and needed to get moving or she would be late opening the store. She could not wait to tell Maggie about her encounter with Miles last night, and knew that her friend would be thrilled. She knew Mags had been secretly and not so secretly praying that she and Miles would become a couple. Ava knew that the "I told you so's" that she would have to endure would be worth it. He was worth it. She grabbed her purse and headed out the door. Today she was turning in her proposal and prayed it would be well received by the landlord.

Maggie beat her to the La Noel and had already brought them their morning caffeine. Ava was a little surprised she had not heard from Miles yet this morning, and hoped he slept well after all the commotion last night. Ava, could not wipe the smile from her face and Maggie immediately zeroed in on her exuberance this morning. *Yes, it was Friday, always a cause for celebration. Check. Yes, she looked fabulous this morning. Check. Yes, she planned to bid on more space that they desperately needed. Check. Yes, she looked like a woman in love. Check. Check!* Maggie grabbed her friend by the shoulders and literally screamed in her face. "O.M.G Ava! You are in love. Finally, you realize you love Miles!"

"What are you psychic? Seriously Mags, is there a video camera in here?" She said looking all around the store room. Maggie grabbed her arm and drug her over to the fainting sofa.

"You are way too happy, elated is the word I would use. Tell me now, tell me everything!" She said sitting crossing her long legs with her foot bobbing up and down in an exaggerated fashion, arms folded across her chest.

"Well I was here late last night and Miles saw my car in the parking lot so he stopped in to check on me. Which was so sweet of him. I asked him to help me get the special angel down out of the attic and he obliged me. While we were on the ladder getting the box down, well, he kissed me."

Maggie let out a screech that could be heard in the next state over. "I knew it!! Finally. Good grief you two took long enough. Thank you Jesus!" She said looking upward and laughing.

"Maggie, seriously it was amazing. He is amazing. I love him, and I know that now. I feel so stupid for having waited so long."

"Oh I'm just saying...I am thrilled for you both. I expect to be the Maid of Honor, I already have the dress."

"Mags of course you will be my Maid of Honor when I decide to get married." She said grinning from ear to ear. "Oh and you are *NOT* wearing that lime green taffeta dress to my wedding. I love you, but that dress is a 'no' go." Maggie walked by with her bottom lip sticking out making Ava laugh even harder. "Pouting will get you nowhere." She shouted after Maggie as she walked towards the counter.

Ava walked past her to turn the open sign in the window and unlock the door, since they were already ten minutes late opening the store. She went back into the office area to retrieve the bid package and looked over it one last time. Her appointment with the landlord was at ten o'clock. She stopped and said another silent prayer for wisdom and grace to accept his decision. Several customers came in all at once, and they were quite busy for the next thirty minutes or so, Ava hoped it would slow down as she didn't want to leave Maggie here alone with a crowd. Thankfully, when it was time for Ava to leave there were only two people still in the store. Maggie blew her a kiss for luck and Ava snatched her portfolio and headed to the landlord's office which was located across the street from her store.

Sebastian stood looking out the Café window and watched as Ava crossed the street. He muttered under his breath viewing her with contempt. He was not sure quite why he felt that way about her, she was easy on the eyes and seemed nice enough, but there was something about her and Miles being together that did not sit well with him. *Jealousy?* He did not believe her to be a gold digger or he would have taken care of that a long time ago. Miles was far too trusting and gave people the benefit of the doubt when it was evident they didn't deserve it. In his opinion, Miles was too soft and it was him that was needed to make sure the family fortune stayed intact.

The mood in the Café was best described as cautious. Word had gotten out about the trouble that Miles had last night with the drunk people, that coupled with Sebastian's presence and the lack of Miles's had given the staff cause for concern. Everyone was doing their best business as usual impression and Sebastian for the most part was staying out of their way.

Miles stopped at a rest area just inside the South Carolina border to stretch his legs. He pulled out his phone and called Ava. Surprisingly it went to voicemail, so then he texted her. *Hi sweetie, unexpected road trip on the way to Atlanta. Long story. I'm just driving, call me when you get a minute. Dying to hear your voice.*

He bought a drink out of the vending machine then got back into the car and turned the car back onto the highway. About fifteen minutes later his phone started ringing, he answered but the voice was not Ava's. "Hey baby! I hear you drew the short straw!" She said laughing at her own joke.

"Candace I am not amused. I had plans today and honestly they did not involve you." He said sternly.

"Miles don't be mean. Mummy and daddy are already cross with me and I might actually be in trouble this time. What time are you going to be here? I want to know if I have time for a mani-pedi."

"G.P.S says I'll be there in approximately three and a half hours. So you better be curb side waiting."

"Fabulous, and I promise I will be, drive safe my knight in shining armor."

"Candy please be ready, I need you to be on time." He hung up as she assured him she would be ready this time. Miles knew that deep down Mr. and Mrs. Weston had hoped one of the Petersen boys would marry their only child Candace, so that their families could be truly joined. Sebastian did not have the patience for her constant drama ridden life, and Miles decided long ago that he work far too hard to invest as much as a dime into that Vegas slot machine of a woman. He loved her, but as a sister, she was so spoiled and over indulged. They all grew up together and knew each other far too well to be anything more than "family". His phone started buzzing again but this time it was Pastor Mark. Now this was a welcome conversation, and Miles was relieved it was him.

Ava left the landlord's office full of hope as he seemed to be sympathetic to her plight and thought she might actually have a shot at the space, regardless of whether the Petersen's were involved or not. She felt confident that they could up with an agreeable solution that would benefit all parties involved. Making her way across the street Ava headed into the Café and scanned the premises for Miles. In her rush to get to her appointment on time, she had left her phone at the store.

She stood over to the side, out of the imaginary official line for service. Soon she was joined by Sebastian, who was looking quite casual today in pressed jeans, and a crisply ironed button down hunter green shirt that caused his eyes to really stand out. He moved very elegantly and cat like, his movements were fluid and stealthy. She imagined he must have been a joy to have around as a child, always sneaking up on everyone.

"Why Miss Turner what do we owe the honor this afternoon? Is there something I can help you with?" Technically his words were honey-like but there was a bite underneath that was slightly unnerving.

"Hello Sebastian, actually I was looking for Miles." She stated, making eye contact briefly with Natasha who quickly looked away and acted busy. Her resent enthusiasm was starting to fade and she began to feel uneasy.

"Oh..." he laughed. "Yes, well Miles is en route to Atlanta to pick up a... friend of his. A very *good* friend." Again the words he spoke were the truth, but the way in which they were delivered insinuated something completely different. Which was his intention, misdirection was his middle name.

"Oh, I see, well I have something for him. May I leave it with you?"

"Certainly. I don't expect him in until later tonight. This may be none of my business, but does this have to do with the building next door?"

"Yes, why?" she tentatively asked.

"Miss Turner, as you must know by now we are also in the market for more space. If we don't get it, well let's just say there will be repercussions. Miles understands this so we are both in agreement and on the same page for once, so to speak. His befriending you and leading you on to get information, as distasteful of a tactic as that may seem, is just business. I hope there will be no hard feelings. Any hopes you have of getting the space, I'm afraid are going to be disappointed. As with Miles, any hopes you had of a future with him, I am afraid are going to be unrealized as well. We are Petersen's and we don't like to lose. Miles did what any man would do in that situation, and he played it to his favor. *Our* favor." Sebastian smiled inwardly as he could see her bottom lip begin to tremble and the large envelope in her hand start shaking. He knew he had her on the ropes, it was that easy.

"Sebastian, are you telling me that Miles's intentions and affections towards me are not true? That it was all for show to get me to tell him what my business plans were? I can't believe he would do that." Her voice trembling now.

"Well you tell me. Has he recently been seeing you more frequently, or has he amped up his attention towards you? Become more affectionate? Again, I am sorry to be the bearer of bad news, Miss Turner. That is why he is not here today, he decided to take the trip to Atlanta to afford himself some distance. I'm sure he considers you as a friend that is just his way, but father has stated he will shut the Café down and move Miles to our Dallas, Texas office if we do not get the space request. Miles did what he had to do. Also, your services will not be needed for the holiday decorations, we have made other arrangements." He took the folder from her hand and held it up stating, "I'll make sure he gets this. Thank you for stopping by." With that, she was dismissed. He turned and sauntered back to the office.

A horrified Natasha would not even look up at Ava and Tim kept his head down, sweeping the same spot on the floor. Ava stood there stunned for a moment then began to feel nauseous. Turning to walk out the door she reached for the handle and a tear escaped, running down her cheek. The morning that had started out with so much promise quickly turned into a storm that was literally breaking her heart. She ran to the La Noel, thankfully there were no customers inside when she entered. Maggie took one look at her face then came running from around the counter to see what was wrong.

Ava was crying so hard by now she could not even speak, so Maggie guided her to the fainting sofa, and sat her down handing her a tissue. "Ava, what happened? Did he turn you down already? Look its ok, we will find a way to deal with the space issues, really honey, its ok."

"Not that." She managed through her sobs.

"Ok, ok, then what? Oh honey, please don't cry." Sitting next to her patting her shoulder.

"Everything with Miles, is a lie! He doesn't *love* me. I am such a fool! Once again I have fallen for a cad." Now her hands covered her face, her shoulders shook she wept so hard.

"No! I don't believe that. Miles *does* love you. I know it. Did *he* tell you that?" Maggie demanded.

"I feel like I'm going to throw up." She said standing, quickly heading for the bathroom closing the door behind her.

Maggie stood there stunned and quickly becoming angry. How dare he mess with her friend like this, she called the Café and Natasha answered.

"What the heck is going on over there Tasha? Ava is a wreck!"

"Mags I can't talk right now. Really. I am so sorry about Ava, truly I am."

"Tasha are you telling me this is true?"

"Maggie I've got to go, I'm sorry. I can't talk." With that said Natasha hung up, she couldn't risk gossiping with Sebastian lurking around. Maggie stood pacing the backroom wondering what in the world was going on and then hearing the jingle bells alerting her that a customer was there. Reluctantly she went back up front to wait on them, and left Ava sobbing in the bathroom.

Natasha walked back into Miles's office to find that Sebastian had opened the envelope that Ava had dropped off. She was quickly learning that he was operating unchecked and that was dangerous.

"What you did to Ava is *so* wrong! Miles is going to be furious and I hope he rips your head off."

Sebastian coolly looked up from the document and then tossed it in the trash bin before he addressed Natasha's outburst with a sly smile.

"Natasha, Miles will hear nothing of this from you or from Tim. Because if I find out that either of you have discussed this with him, I will not only fire you both but I make sure that you will never work again this side of Kansas." Stepping closer with a menacing stare he got very close to her face, speaking in an icy tone "Are we very clear on this point? You will keep your mouths shut."

Wide eyed, she merely nodded slowly and hesitantly walked backwards out of the office. *Poor Ava. Poor Miles! How am I going to be able to do my job and not tell Miles what is going on?* Unfortunately as much as she respected Miles, she felt he was no match for Sebastian and his wicked ways. She was not convinced Miles would be able to protect her if Sebastian made good on his threat.

Chapter 6

Boondoggle

Finally pulling up to the address on the G.P.S. Miles found Candace waiting on him like she promised. He was stunned. He put the car in park, left it running then quickly popped the trunk latch and got out to help her with her bags. She looked no worse for wear in her skinny jeans that made her legs look a mile long, her nails were painted and her long blonde hair perfectly in place. However, she did look a little tired. He grabbed her four suitcases and loaded them in the back of the Mercedes. Then opened her door for her so she could enter in, she hugged him first, placed a quick peck on the cheek, then slid into the seat. He shut the door then made his way back around and got in the driver's side.

"Wow I was terrified you were going to show up in the old Land Rover. This is awesome."

"Thank father, it was his idea. If it had been left up to me I would have driven the barn truck."

"Oh Miles, surely you don't mean that? Good heavens."

"So are you going to tell me what's going on and why I'm on this boondoggle?" He stated flatly.

"Miles, I've messed up and my life is in shambles." She said sounding a little dramatic.

"Is this the kind of trouble that can be bought with money, or the life changing kind?"

"A bit of both, I'm afraid."

"Spill it."

"Miles please don't judge me, ok?"

"Candace you are like a sister to me. I was there when you were born and even held you when you were hours old. We grew up together. I love you and nothing will ever change that. Nothing. However, I do not always like the choices you make, and I want what is best for you. That's all. I can't help you if I don't know what I am up against."

Miles tried hard to mentally prepare for what she would say, and he hoped he would not respond in a reactionary manner.

"Ok. I am failing school Miles. *Fashion design.* How do you *fail* fashion design? Also the reason my car is totaled is because I went to a party, drank too much and missed a turn then crashed into a tree. Thankfully I just had a bump on my head, but the car is toast. So now I have a DUI on my record, and no car. Lastly and please don't say I told you so.... but well, Rob and I broke up. Turns out he *was* seeing other people and well his parting gift to me was an STD!"

Miles nearly wrecked the car when he heard that one, and had to remind himself to breathe. He had never liked Rob. Miles knew he was a player, but now he seriously wanted to physically rip him a new one.

"Thankfully it's one that can be treated with antibiotics so it will eventually go away. The stigma of that is just about unbearable. Plus I was so angry when I found out he was cheating, then about the STD I lost it and trashed his car with a golf club. So now I have a destroying private property charge against me," she finished then leaned her head against the window and looked at the cars as they passed by.

Miles reached over taking her hand and holding it for a moment. "Candy, I want you to listen to me. Carefully."

"Miles please don't preach to me. I know I am a screw up, just don't kick me while I'm down." Being just a little too melodramatic for his taste.

"Candace Renee Weston, you had better look at me and hear me." Candy slowly looked over at him and gave him her full attention.

"First of all, let's look at all the positives. Number one, even if you do fail out of school your family is wealthy enough to take care of you. Ninety percent of the people in the United States cannot boast of that, so be grateful. Number two, you seriously could have been killed or worse, killed an innocent person with that drunk driving stunt. Be grateful you escaped with little more than a bump on your head. In regards to Rob and that situation, again you were spared a disease that you could have carried for the rest of your life! As far as the property damage goes, that can be addressed easily. So again, no lives lost, be grateful! I am not trying to minimize your angst, but we have established there is a lot for you to be grateful for here, despite your bad decisions. Candy you are living under the borrowed grace of God through people who believe, love and pray for you. I know you believe there is a God, but do you truly know Him?"

She cast her eyes down, pulled her hand back into her lap and stared straight ahead. Miles shifted in his seat and turned the radio off. Traffic was getting heavy and he needed to pay attention, Atlanta at rush hour was a nightmare.

Miles started again, "Candy, listen I am not trying to beat you up about this, but I have an idea I think you need to seriously consider. When we get to the house I want you to go in first thing and apologize to your parents. They deserve a sincere apology. You have wasted your father's hard earned money by not applying yourself in college, by over shopping, partying, and by wrecking the car he provided for you, which was a nice vehicle. Your mother deserves an apology for all the worry you have put her through. Secondly, I want you to take a semester or two off from school because I want you to get a job. A real job. Perhaps you could come work for me at the Café? The other thing is you need to be able to live off of what you make. No subsides from mommy and daddy. Work around people with real life issues and day to day struggles. You need a different perspective Candace, a reality check of sorts."

"Ok. Ok, Miles. Do you really think it will make a difference?"

"Absolutely. The carefree socialite party girl life is over, you are an adult now Candy and you need some real life skills. Plus, if you are up for it you can go to church with me and Ava."

"Ok, I guess that would be ok. I've met Ava before right?"

"Yes you may have seen her before, but I am not sure you have been formally introduced. I'll see that it happens. You will absolutely love her, she is great."

Which reminded him he had not heard from her all day. He checked his phone again and no text or returned call. Candace put the seat back closing her eyes since they were stuck in traffic, and thought she would rest a bit. Baring your soul is such hard work. They were still inside the Atlanta beltway where there were five lanes of North bound traffic, bumper to bumper. The car was literally at a standstill, and the large electronic highway sign indicated there were two wrecks ahead of them. This was going to be a long ride home, he could already tell. He called his parents to update them on the return time so they would not be concerned.

Next he called the Café to see how the day was going and if Sebastian was still there. Katie answered and indicated the morning shift was uneventful, and that she was feeling ok after last night. She stated that although Sebastian had gone home for a few hours that he would be back later this evening. Miles was pleased to hear that he would be back before closing. Although he did not anticipate a repeat of what happened last night, he felt better knowing that Sebastian would be there in case anything came up. Sebastian came across as a suit, a stuffy business man, but what few people knew was that he was an accomplished athlete and a proficient black belt who had studied under some of the best sensei.

Lastly he called the La Noel and Maggie answered. She was curt, briefly stating that Ava had gone home sick. He was concerned but now it made sense as to why he had not heard from her all day. Since they were stopped in traffic he sent a quick text, *Ava, I am so sorry you feel bad, get some rest and if you are feeling better later give me a call.-Miles.*

Miles felt exhaustion starting to creep in and he was struggling to stay awake. They were finally free of the accidents and traffic was moving once again. He decided to stop at the next exit to get them something to eat. Candace was awake now and they decided to go inside instead of driving through the drive through window. Standing up and walking around should be enough to wake him up. He and

Candy ate dinner, chatting casually for about forty five minutes then they got back on the road.

The further north they drove the colder it became, and the weather report stated a cold front with precipitation was headed their way. The possibility of snow was in the forecast for the following week, November was coming in strong and the forecast of snow before Thanksgiving was uncommon.

Miles stopped at the edge of town to top off the gas in his father's car then pulled into the gate around 9:45 p.m. The traffic in Atlanta had really slowed down their progress. Miles carried in Candace's luggage and set it down in his old room which his mother had converted into another guest bedroom. Their parents were in the living room playing cards but all paused when they heard them enter in through the back door. The Petersen's went into the kitchen and the Weston's stayed in the living room. Miles sat at the breakfast bar while Candace went on in to see her parents.

Mr. Petersen extended his hand to Miles shaking it firmly as an unspoken thank you. His mother came around to him and gently brushed his hair out of his face, and kissed him on the cheek. "Thank you sweetheart for picking her up. It means more than you will ever know."

"Father I have refueled your car and its back in the garage. Thank you for letting me take it, I'm not sure the Rover would have been up for the trip. It needs servicing."

"Of course son, I would not have asked you to take such a trip and not provide for you. Please let me know what the gas bill was and I will reimburse you."

"Yes sir. Well, if you will both excuse me I am beat."

"Honey have you eaten supper?"

"Yes ma'am. We stopped at a restaurant right outside of Atlanta."

"Alright then, we will see you tomorrow. Don't forget the Halloween party is tomorrow night and we are expecting you. Please bring a friend if you like." she said smiling. He nodded and waved goodbye.

He looked down and checked his phone again as he walked to the cottage, still there was nothing from Ava. She must be feeling really poorly and that made him miserable to think that she was sick and he was not there to care for her. He texted her one last time before he went to bed. *You must be feeling really badly, and I feel terrible that I am not there to take care of you. Call me tomorrow and let me know how you are.-Miles*

Lying there in bed, Ava was exhausted from crying all day. She had received a couple of texts from Miles and that made the situation even more confusing. *Was he still playing the game, not knowing that Sebastian had already given him up? Or was he being sincere?* She was absolutely heartbroken and ashamed to think she had been played by Miles and Sebastian. How would she ever face the staff in the Café again after Sebastian said all of that in front of Natasha and Tim? The humiliation was crushing. Their lives were already so intertwined with church and their work, separation was going to prove to be painful and difficult.

She took a couple more Advil, laid back down and turned off all the lights. Perhaps things would look clearer in the morning.

Miles opened up the Café and he was actually glad to be back at work, he missed his routine and missed seeing Ava. Natasha came in about five minutes after him, and was not her usual chipper self. She was acting distant and guarded.

"Hey Tasha, Good Morning."

"Hey." She said scooting past him, not making eye contact.

"How did everything go yesterday with Sebastian being here?"

"Fine." As she walked past Miles tying on her apron.

"Are you ok? Did something happen yesterday that I need to know about?"

"Nope." She said curtly as she began grinding the coffee beans.

Miles went into his office and looked at yesterday's deposits along with the mail that came in, then he went out and spoke to Tim and got a very similar reaction to Natasha's. *What in the heck happened here yesterday, the mood in here is grim?*

He decided to give them both some space and see how the morning went. He called Sebastian and got a relatively civil greeting, which should have been another red flag.

"Hey how did it go yesterday? Any problems or issues I need to know about?"

"No, the staff was a little unsure of me being there all day. Things were fine and it was quiet last night; no problems at all. How was the drive down and back?"

"Aside from hideous traffic in the Atlanta area, it was relatively uneventful."

"Ok, well I have to run and get a few things for mother before the party tonight. See you later."

Miles sat there running his hands through his hair wondering what dimension he had stepped into because everything in his world seemed upside down. His loyal staff was acting distant and his petulant brother was acting decent, that coupled with missing Ava made him feel off balance and wary. He prayed she was feeling better today and that she would give him a call.

Maggie opened the store this morning then came in early for her latte. Miles was still in the office so he didn't see her, so Natasha waited on her but was quiet and didn't make a lot of eye contact. "Tasha, what's going on here? Is Miles going to be here today?"

"He's in the back and honestly I can't even look at him. It's going to be a long morning, I just hope we are busy up until he leaves at two today. I'm not sure I could carry on a conversation with him at this point, so I'm just going to keep my head down and stay busy."

"So it's true? Oh my God, Ava was right. Bless her heart, I could literally kill him right now. Where is he going at two today?"

"His mother's annual Halloween costume party. He and Sabastian are setting it up for her, I hear it's a blast and the prize for the winner is like two or three hundred dollars."

"Ugg, I totally forgot today is Halloween! I have been so distracted with Ava and the store. I am working our church's trunk or treat event tonight. Well Ava called in "sick" today so I have it all to myself. She is struggling so much, it's heartbreaking."

"I hate that, I really do. I'm not sure if I can continue to work under these oppressive conditions, and I may have to find a new job myself." Natasha said in a low voice. They both waved goodbye as Maggie headed back down to La Noel.

After dusting the store and vacuuming she sat down for a few minutes and Natasha's words came back to her. *Why would Tasha have to find a new job? Miles may have used Ava to advance his business goals, which is despicable, but she has never known him to ever be unkind, let alone oppressive to any of his staff. What could she be talking about? Natasha loved the Café and more importantly she loved Miles as a boss. Something else is going on....*

Miles came out of his office and announced he was going to run a couple of errands. Miles overheard the portion of their conversation that Ava was still not feeling well. Aside from being sick he figured she must also be worried about the building next door. Natasha waived him off, stating she would call if they needed him and for him to take his time. He swung by the church and met with Pastor Mark for about an hour. He had indicated during their conversation on his way to Atlanta that he wanted to discuss his evolving relationship with Ava. Now he wanted to discuss the situation with Candace, he valued Mark's counsel and wanted them to pray together over these issues.

Afterwards, he stopped by Dot's diner to get Ava some vegetable soup and take it over to her house. He was dying to see her and hoped the soup would make her feel better.

Ava made her way into the kitchen, attempted to make some toast and poured some apple juice into a small glass. She took one small sip causing her stomach to heave so she left that and the toast on the countertop. She had not eaten anything since she spoke to Sebastian yesterday. Even though she had no appetite, she thought she should try and eat a little something. Her head was pounding from all the crying, and she still felt queasy. Ava knew she needed to pull it together and soon, since she had a business to run. However, she literally felt as though her heart was being ripped in two.

Laying there last night she kept going back and forth in her mind. Feeling one minute there is no way that Miles would do this to her, and then the next feeling she knew his love and their relationship was too good to be true. Satan playing on all her fears and insecurities. After wrestling with those thoughts for the remainder of the day into the night, she finally got out her Bible and started reading. Ava was pouring out her heart to God pleading with him to make the hurt go away. She had received Miles's last text but didn't respond. What should she say? What could she say? The thought of seeing him anytime soon nearly took her breath away, she just needed time to process all of this pain.

With her phone in her hand she started towards the stairs when her doorbell rang. She set her phone on the foyer table and opened the door thinking maybe Maggie had come by to bring her lunch. Much to her surprise there stood Miles. He had a concerned look on his face and a small bag in his hand that he handed to her.

"Hey, I don't want to keep you, I know you don't feel well, but I thought you might like some of Dot's homemade soup." She took it from him trying not to look him in the eye and set it on the foyer table.

"Uh thanks." She feebly managed. Seeing him made her feel as though all the air was leaving her lungs and she began to feel dizzy. The next thing she saw was Miles rushing towards her—then nothing.

Miles swooped in a caught her before she hit the floor. The look on her face when she opened the door was telling and thankfully he was ready. He lifted her slight frame up as though she were a small sleeping child and held her close to his chest kissing her on the forehead. He walked through her den and kitchen into an area he thought might be her bedroom. If memory served him correctly, when she was telling him about the renovations a while back, she had mentioned that she liked her bedroom being on the main floor. So it had to be here somewhere.

Still cradling her close to him looking downward he noticed her face was puffy, and that her eyes looked swollen and her nose chapped from constant blowing he surmised. He thought she had a stomach virus from what Maggie had indicated, but perhaps she had developed a head cold too, or worse the flu?

He located her bedroom, laid her gently on the bed and covered her up. Miles noticed her bible was at the foot of her bed along with about thirty tissues in the small trash can nearby. He went into her bathroom and found a washcloth then ran some cool water over it, then rang it out and tenderly placed it over her swollen eyes. She stirred slightly as he knelt down beside her bed and brushed the hair out of her face. He didn't want to be standing over her when she awoke and startle her. She tried to open her eyes, then he placed his hand over hers.

"Shhh. Ava, just rest. You fainted, and I bet you haven't eaten much since you've been sick." He said in a soothing calm voice.

"No... Miles, you can't be here..." she started and faded.

"I know, I'm not staying, but I am worried about you. I will put the soup in the kitchen, promise me you will eat some after you have rested."

She managed a weak nod. He tucked her in gently, then adjusted the cloth on her eyes and sweetly placed a kiss on her forehead. He retrieved the soup then placed it in the refrigerator and left her a note on the counter begging her to call him or Maggie if she felt worse. One of them would take her to the doctor. He made sure the house was secure before he locked the front door, then went out the side door that would automatically lock when he closed it. She looked horrible and so very fragile, it grieved him to see her in this condition.

He stopped back by the Café to check on them one last time before he headed back to the estate to help set up for tonight's activities. His heart was not into this party, he was hoping to duck out early and just be alone. He had a lot on his mind plus he was worried about Ava.

CHAPTER 7

Halloween

Arriving at the house, Miles started setting up tables and chairs then he began arranging the sound system. Sebastian left the estate early to pick up his date, a new woman he was seeing causally and promised to be back by the time the party started at seven. Miles assumed Candy would be his date tonight since they were both flying solo this year. She was going as Glenda, the Good Witch from the Wizard of OZ, and this year he was going as an F.B.I. agent. Usually his parents also dressed up but it was their year to judge, so they would be in regular attire. Every year a different couple was selected to judge, usually whoever had won the previous year had the honors.

Miles had a couple of hours before the party started so he decided to take a long hot shower and a nap. His mind drifted to Ava, and he longed to be over there with her. The weather had turned really cold so there was a chill in the cottage. He covered up on the couch with a blanket with Zelda the faithful lying at his feet. Nothing like a forty five pound dog to keep your feet warm when you are cold.

He woke about an hour or so later when Zelda launched off the couch and began pacing in front of the door her nails clicking on the hard wood floors. "Z. What's up girl? Who's outside?" It had to be someone she knew otherwise she would be barking up a storm. Reluctantly he got up, looking out the window and saw Candy making her way up the walk.

He opened the door before she had a chance to knock.

"Hey what's up? Does mom need something?"

"Hey. Oh no, we're good, I've been helping quite a bit and I think we have it under control. The caterers just left and everything is set. Max and Ellen are going to be the Valet's tonight and park everyone at the barn. So we are in good shape."

"I didn't realize Max was back in town. When did that happen?"

"Your mom heard from him this week I think, and invited them out. I hear he is wanting to move back here near Mapleton, since he is not happy in Kentucky."

"Ok. Well good. I'll have to go down and see him then. We spoke a couple of weeks ago and he never mentioned coming down for a visit."

"I think it's just a quick trip, but he said he was coming back for Thanksgiving."

"OK, well that's just a few short weeks away."

"Miles I love you and I want you to know that. Mom and daddy were right to send you to get me in Atlanta. I want to apologize to you for being such a pain, and for hijacking your day yesterday. I apologized to them both and we all cried. I told them what you said to me about school and a job, and they think it's a great idea. Your parents have agreed to let me stay for a semester or two here at the house so I can start whenever you are ready for me."

"Candace I am proud of you. This won't be easy and I know that, but I promise if you work hard and go in with the right attitude it will make a huge difference."

"Well thanks for not giving up on me Miles. That means more to me than anything, that you care enough to call me out and set me straight." With that said she stood up smiling then stuck her fist out and they bumped.

"Ok now get out of here I have to get dressed, and so do you since you are my date tonight."

"Oh yeah? What about Ava, I thought you invited her?"

"No, I think she has the flu or something, at any rate she is really sick. So I am going solo." He walked her to the door and then went into the bedroom to finish getting dressed. He checked his phone, still nothing from Ava, but he had one text from Sebastian asking about a wine, and that was it. Miles walked down to the barn and visited with his old friend Max and his wife. They didn't have much time to visit since guests started arriving and Max was parking cars before the party. They agreed to catch up at Thanksgiving.

The party went off without a hitch and the neighbors down the street took home the prize for best costume, they came as Ben Franklin and Betsy Ross. The food was exceptional this year and the crowd was a decent size probably forty couples and a few singles. Everyone disbursed around midnight but Miles managed to sneak away just before eleven. He got into bed then began to pray before he fell asleep and slept soundly through the night.

Ava woke up about eight p.m. and thought she had dreamed that Miles came by to see her. In it he was sweet and gentle making her long for him even more. She padded into the kitchen and her knees buckled when she saw his note. *He was here! It wasn't a dream, oh dear Lord and he saw me like this?* She opened the refrigerator and retrieved the soup he had left and warmed it in the microwave. She finally had a bit of appetite and the soup was light and should sit well on her stomach. After eating about a cup of the soup she went into the bathroom and brushed her hair out and then brushed her teeth. Her head was still throbbing but not as badly since she had eaten some soup. She laid back down falling asleep almost immediately and awoke abruptly about 1:30 a.m.

She decided to text Miles back. *Thank you for the soup. It helped. ~ Ava*

Regardless of how much he had deceived her, she was not going to sink to a level that was uncivil and rude. After all he did bring it by, either out of concern or guilt she did not know which. She laid back down trying to remember his visit but it was so hazy she could not recall the events. Lying there she reminisced about their time together Thursday night and a single tear slid down her cheek. Just when she thought she could not possibly have any more tears left, one by one they trailed down her face. She rolled over trying her best to forget that Thursday ever happened, and push Miles out of her mind.

Miles woke up the next morning and saw her text. With his heart pounding his chest, hoping she was feeling better and that he would see her at church today. He dressed, rushed through breakfast with his family and left for church early. He stayed in the sanctuary praying for the service, for his family, for Candace and for Ava. He also prayed that God would help him to live out the verses that had been laid on his heart over the last two weeks. His men's Sunday school class was studying Matthew and the Sermon on the Mount. However, two verses in particular kept haunting him and he felt like God was trying to make a point. Although Miles did not quite understand what the point was, he felt God must have a reason and he prayed God would make that clear to him. The verses were Matthew 5vs 7-8. *Blessed are the merciful for they shall obtain mercy, and blessed are the pure in heart for they shall see God.*

After Sunday school his heart sank when he entered the sanctuary for services and Ava was not there. He sat in their regular spot longing to see her. The sermon was one that pricked his heart, it was about loving God and about 'right' relationships and about how you cannot have one apart from God. It was a powerful message and two lost souls were saved at the end of the service. One was a fairly new kid he had worked with in the youth group recently, so that was certainly a cause for celebration.

Maggie was stunned and elated to see Ava at her church this morning. Maggie attended First Baptist in downtown Mapleton, the enormous church with grand white pillars and a steeple you could see from space. They were '*very proud*' Maggie jokingly would say. The two women hugged and sat together as the preacher preached on forgiveness. As followers of Christ we are called to forgive, regardless of the wrong, since Christ forgave us in our trespasses and sins. It was a powerful message and one that punched Ava right in the gut. Maggie picking up on that sentiment reached across and held Ava's hand.

When church ended, Maggie invited Ava out to lunch with her family. They were going into the city to run a couple of errands and were going to eat while they were out. Ava hesitated and just wanted to go home, but before she knew it Maggie had placed her into the car and they were on the road. A Christian kidnapping of sorts but with fried chicken involved. Ava was assured it would all be just fine, it actually felt good to get out of the house and Maggie could always make Ava laugh. She needed to get her mind off Miles for a few hours. She knew she wanted to be at church today, but just could not face walking into her church and seeing Miles there. Ava knew she was going to have to face him eventually, but she just needed a little more time.

Miles solemnly left church and went to the Café. They were closed on Sundays and he wanted to tidy up the office and do some deep cleaning. He had been looking to purchase new furniture and needed to assess his current floor plan to see if the new pieces would even work. So he took out his sketch pad and started walking around the store marking the placement of tables and usable space. As he was flipping the pages to get to a clean one and came across a sketch he had started of Ava a few months back. She had taken a seat at one of the tables near the window, sitting there with her beverage, and was gazing out into the street as people passed by her. The way the sunlight caught in her hair was amazing and he had to get it on paper, so he had sketched her from the coffee bar.

He often thought about the fact that he was in love with someone who did *not* drink coffee at all, and he laughed at the irony. She claimed she loved the way it smelled, but had never acquired a taste for it. So he and Katie spent hours trying to find a coffee, latte, cappuccino, or something that would appeal to her delicate palate, only to miserably strike out. So they accepted their defeat, and created Ava her very own special hot chocolate that was designed for her taste buds. During the summer months Ava would come in the Café for a soda or juice drink, but when October came, she started back with the hot chocolates. It was one of the many little things he loved about her.

He called Ava's phone but it went to voice mail. *Hi Ava, it's Miles. I hope you are feeling better today, I got your text, and I'm glad that it helped out. I miss you something fierce. Please get well soon, I need to talk to you about something and I really don't want to do it over the phone. Ok, take care....bye.*

He sat staring at the sketch and made up his mind right then that he had to get this on a canvas. He abandoned his cleaning quest and drove home to set his art studio up again. This is one of the many things that Miles and his mother share, a love and talent for art. Originally the cottage was used as Mary Beth's art / music studio when the boys were younger, so when Miles moved in after college, she left it there for him. She had seasons where she would paint daily, then seasons where she wouldn't pick up a brush for months at a time, that was just her way.

Maggie and Ava had a great time with Maggie's family. Maggie's mother was a hoot, and her father had a very dry sense of humor so both together made Ava's stomach hurt from laughing so hard. Maggie also had an older sister Hannah, who was a missionary in Europe and the Ukraine. She was home for now visiting churches sharing her ministry, and raising money to go back. She was also able to join them for lunch and Ava enjoyed getting to see her again. Ava remembered how cool and fearless she and Maggie thought Hannah was being five years their senior. Hearing about her life now and everything that she is involved with Ava decided that they were correct in their initial assessment. Hannah is fearless and cool, but so very humble giving God all the glory for her mission work and victories over there. After lunch, everyone hugged and had to go their separate ways, so Ava made sure she got Hannah's email address so that they could personally stay in touch.

"Thanks girl for the lunch and laughs today I needed it desperately, and I am so sorry I just left you with the store. Please forgive me."

"Hey, not a problem, I am just sorry you have been so upset. Rightfully so of course. What are you going to do Ava? I saw Natasha yesterday and she is so upset about something that she may even look for another job."

"What? Why? Miles would be devastated if she left."

"I know! She said something about not being able to work in such an oppressive environment."

"That just doesn't make sense. Unless Sebastian is taking over, surely that is not the case?"

The drive back to Mapleton went by quickly as they chatted the whole way home. Spending time with Maggie was better than a therapist and a whole lot cheaper.

Maggie dropped Ava back off at the church so she could get her car. Once she arrived at the house, she realized she had a message from Miles. She sat on the couch covering her legs with her afghan then playing the message. Hearing his voice made her stomach do flip flops and she put the phone up to her forehead playing it over and over. Ava had a feeling she knew what he wanted to talk about.... Only she didn't know if she could actually bear to hear the words come out of his mouth. It was bad enough hearing it from Sebastian, and she knew in her heart she could not possibly endure hearing it from him.

Sitting up dialing his number, she took a deep breath, and after several rings his voice mail picked up. *Miles I think I know what you are going to say and honestly it's not necessary. I get it. This was all just business and you are moving on. I would appreciate if you didn't call or text me anymore, it's just too hard on me. Maybe one day we can be friends again, but for now I just need space to sort everything out. Thanks.*

Ava ended the call then drew and nice hot bath with scented oils. She soaked in the tub with her eyes closed and stayed until the water cooled and her fingers were pruned. She donned her pajamas then crawled into bed. She was trying so hard to make sense of the mess that was now her life. Tomorrow was another day, and she just hoped that Miles would heed her request and leave her alone.

Working in the studio, Miles made good headway on starting the portrait. He looked down at Zelda who was stretched out sound asleep near his easel. He stretched his long arms then walked into the kitchen in search of food. The clock showed the time as 11:15p.m. No wonder he was stiff and starving! He rummaged through the refrigerator and found some leftovers from the party in there boxed up. Candace or his mother must have brought them over for him, he made a mental note to hug them both when he saw them next. He fixed a plate then eagerly ate the entire thing. He reached over and checked his phone, there was a text from Candace and a voicemail from Ava left around 8:30 p.m.

It was too late to call her back tonight, he would have to talk to her tomorrow. He played the voicemail and anxiously awaited to hear her voice. Listening to the message he was feeling confused. He felt like he had been punched in the gut, he stumbled backwards into the kitchen chair and replayed it. None of it made any sense at all and it was almost as if the message was truly meant for someone else.

What did she mean that she knew what I was going to say? And that I have moved on? Moved on to what?

He stood, then paced back and forth trying to make sense of her message. *Could she possibly think that when I went to Atlanta to get Candy that I was moving on? Surely not! Doesn't she know me any better than that? None of this makes any sense at all! I will speak to her tomorrow and get all this straighten out.*

He thought back to when he was at her house, and the way her eyes looked with all the tissues, had she been crying? Is that why she would not return his texts? Was she was under some misguided perception that he did not love or care for her? He collapsed back on to the couch and put his head in his hands. *No! This could not be happening.* He would not let a misunderstanding derail their relationship, and he was crushed to think she did not know him any better. He felt sick inside and longed for the morning so that he could make things right.

CHAPTER 8

Driven

Ava arrived at the store just in time to open, she had stopped at a McDonald's to get hot chocolate this morning and was running a little behind. Miles on the other hand woke up at four a.m., showered and went into the Café early. He made sure everything was set up properly for the morning crowd then completed the cleaning he had abandoned yesterday. Natasha came in bewildered as to why he was there so early, noting he barely spoke to anyone. He moved like a man on a mission and his attitude was one of determination.

When 9:15 rolled around he dropped his cleaning cloth in the sink washed his hands, and walked out of the Café and down to La Noel. Ava saw him when he reached the edge of the window, turned and ran out the back door. She knew this was ridiculous behavior but she was not up for a confrontation. Miles walked in and got Maggie instead.

"Hey Maggie, is Ava around? I saw her car out back."

"Sorry Miles she just left for the bank." She stated off handedly with her head down acting as though she was busy checking paperwork.

"I really need to talk to her Maggie. It's important." His voice catching a bit. That got Maggie's attention, and when she looked up at him, her stomach dropped. He looked as bad as Ava, like he had not slept in days. His normally bright eyes had dark circles, he was unshaven and his hair was slicked back and kicked up at his collar.

"She's really not here Miles. I'm sorry."

"Maggie Please." He paused for a moment with his hands on his hips, "Please tell her I came by and she's got it all wrong. There has been some kind of big misunderstanding." Then he turned and walked out of the store. Maggie exhaled bracing herself against the counter top.

Miles called Ava and it went to her voicemail. *Ava, it's Miles, I'm not sure what's going on but there has been some kind of miscommunication. Please let me clear it up, I really don't understand what's going on. Please let's talk in person. I need to see you.*

Ava saw his call come through and let it go to voicemail. She did not want to fight with him, or put him in a position where he felt like he had to lie to cover Sebastian. Not to mention she did not want to say anything that she would regret. She was starting to move past the hurt phase and into the anger and indignation phase. She didn't know if she liked this phase any better than the last, but at least she was not crying 24/7 anymore. So that was an improvement.

Miles came back to the Café and paced around like a lion stalking imaginary prey. He could not seem to sit for any length of time and his conversations were short and terse. Natasha wanted so badly to take him in the office and tell him what had happened so he could fix it. If it was even fixable? However, with the mood he was in, she was afraid if he found out what Sebastian had done, he would start busting up furniture or something. Finally after pacing around making the staff nervous, and constantly looking at his phone he announced "I'm going for a run, I don't know when I'll be back. Call me if anything important happens, like the building catches fire or something."

"We'll handle anything that comes up." Natasha offered. Miles nodded and was off.

Both of the Petersen boys were athletes, Miles had played football and ran track in high school and college. Sebastian played soccer in school, and now runs in marathons. Miles usually ran a couple times a week to stay in shape, but Sebastian ran every day, and he was extremely disciplined. Miles retrieved his sweats out of the Rover and changed in the Café. He warmed up and then took off towards the park, to clear his head.

The weather had certainly taken a turn for the worse, as the wind bit into his face and hands, turning them red and chapping them. When he passed by the bank the time and temperature sign stated it was a balmy 27 degrees. The wind made it feel much colder, but he pressed onward as though hell hounds were chasing him.

After Ava returned to the store Maggie filled her in on Miles's visit and they both agreed that something was not right. Tugging at her heart again that maybe he was for real, and Sebastian for whatever reason, was just being a jerk. Perhaps that is what Sebastian would have done, so he assumed Miles would behave the same way? Unfortunately, neither of them had enough experience with Sebastian to know how he would respond one way or another, but they did know Miles and they both felt like this was way out of character for him.

"I'm going to call him, but I can't meet tonight since I'm gone all week. I guess it will have to be Friday or Saturday."

She picked up her phone and dialed his number. His voicemail picked up. *"Hi Miles, I got your message, and I think we do need to meet and talk. Unfortunately I can't do it before Friday. I am leaving for a business trip and I won't be back until then, so why don't I just meet you at the Café Saturday morning? Text me and let me know if that works. Well, ok....um, Bye."* She pressed END and slid the phone in her purse.

"Thanks for taking the store for me this week, is Hannah still coming over to help you for a few days?" she asked as she gathered her things.

"Yeah, she'll be here at noon, and then she is going to spend a couple of days with me. Call me when you get to Charlotte and let me know you arrived safely. If you can, try to leave the trade show a little early, this weather is horrible and they are calling for a winter snow storm or worse...ice, this weekend." Maggie cautioned.

After saying goodbye Ava headed out to her loaded down SUV. This was a holiday-home trade show they always attended right after Halloween and usually did very well. Maggie was right, normally early November weather was not quite this "wintery" and it was certainly going to make getting home interesting. She drove past the Mexican restaurant that she and Miles had eaten at on her way out of town, and it made her feel a little sad... Perhaps this trade show trip was coming at a good time after all. At the very least she would be extremely busy and would not have time to think about Miles.

After running nearly five miles through the park and around town, Miles made it back to his vehicle. He located his keys then decided to head home for a hot soak and some lunch. He looked over at his phone and saw he had missed a call from Ava. Quickly he listened to her message and for the first time in twenty four hours he felt hopeful. He still was not sure what was going on with everyone, Ava, Maggie and his brother all acting so odd. That along with the fact his staff was completely avoiding him, perhaps Saturday he would get the answers he so desperately sought. *Saturday seems a life time away.* Either way it was going to be a very long week.

Miles arrived at the estate and as he drove past the main house saw that his father's car was home. He stopped abruptly, threw the Rover into Park, and hopped out. He entered through the garage and made his way down the long marble hallway that led to his father's office. His mother was sitting in the library reading when he whisked by, "Miles, sweetheart?" she called after him. He stopped and backed up until he was in the doorway of the library, "Yes ma'am?"

"Honey where are you going in such a rush dressed like that? Are you ok?" She inquired. He was still in his sweaty mismatched running clothes and tennis shoes. She could tell Miles had something on his mind and it concerned her. Normally they were very close, but lately he was quiet and more withdrawn.

"I'm on my way to speak with father, and actually I think I would like you to be present too, if you have time?"

She closed her book, stood and reached out for his hand. He took it, grinned and gave her hand a squeeze, as they proceeded down the hall to his father's home office. Miles stepped ahead of her taking the lead and lightly knocked on his father's door. Thomas Petersen looked up from his laptop, "Why Miles, this is a pleasant surprise, and Mary Beth! To what do I owe this honor you two?"

"Father I know you are busy and this is rather impromptu, but I have had this on my heart and I just can't sit on it any longer. I asked mother to sit in since Sebastian is not here, what I have to say concerns him as well. Do you have time to speak with me now?"

Miles loved his father and had always tried so desperately to get his attention. He played football because he thought it would please his father, went to the same college as his father in hopes of establishing some kind of bond. Yet there always seemed to be distance between them. While Sebastian seemed to be his father's favorite and they bonded over almost everything it seemed from food, to wine, movies, sports, and of course business. It was always unspoken but understood that Sebastian was the heir apparent and honestly Miles was ok with that. However, he did long to have his father's time and affection. Mary Beth realized this and it broke her heart to see him trying so hard.

"Son if you feel it is that important, then please come in and have a seat."

"Thank you." he sat down and tried not to fidget. There was something about being in his father's office that made him feel like a ten year old child in trouble. The office was decorated in rich wood tones with dark brown leather seats in front of the desk and a small taupe leather sofa against one wall. The pictures that hung on the walls were oil paintings of ships on the ocean, some on calm waters, and some in the middle of tempests. *Art imitating life* his father used to say.

"I'll just be direct. Mom, dad I would like to have full control of the Café. I have worked my tail off for the last four and a half years, getting up at 4:30 or 5:00 a.m. every morning to open, and sometimes staying until closing. I handle the staff, the ordering, I do the books, payroll, taxes, clean toilets and scrub floors. I can and have done it all. Not only can I run the day to day operations, but I have established some firm relationships in the community promoting the business and also helping the other business by cross selling products. By doing this I have saved the Café money while helping fellow small business men with their businesses. I am proud of the work I have done there, and not only have I turned it into a great place to hang out and meet, but I have turned a profit. A steady profit where each quarter is better than the last and annually we are the best we have been since we opened."

His father sat there with his hands folded listening, giving Miles his undivided attention. His mother sat on the edge of her seat, silently cheering him onward.

"I know that Sebastian is technically in charge of the Café business, but I feel like I have earned the right to take it over permanently. If you would like Sebastian to stay on and check the books behind me that would be acceptable, but I feel I deserve to have the Café. I know you had hopes of me working in the Dallas office, but father, it is not what I want. I want you to know that I appreciate *everything* you have ever done, or provided for us as a family. So many things I could never repay. I have simple needs, I don't require a lot of the finery that Sebastian enjoys and that is not meant as a slight in anyway. We are just different, and I love the people at the Café, my customers, being in a small town and what it affords. This is not just a whim, I've been praying about it for a long time now."

Pausing, catching his breath, started again "I don't know if I'm even making sense." Miles sat there staring at his father, scanning for a reaction.

"Miles I appreciate you sharing your feelings with me, and I do hear what you are saying. I have seen the numbers and they do corroborate your brief assessment. Although the numbers are a large part of the business, what means more to me than the profit margin right now, is your passion for the business. I would be remiss if I said I was not somewhat disappointed in your reluctance to join in the family business, but I also know putting a square peg in a round hole never works. Miles I am proud of you and what you have accomplished with this small business. You took the work seriously, none of it was ever treated as if it was beneath you, and the long hours did not go unnoticed. Please allow me time to think this through and I will give you my decision by the end of the week. Is that acceptable to you?"

"Yes. Of course. Thank you." Miles stated relieved.

"Is there anything else you would like to talk about?"

"No sir. I am in desperate need of a shower." He said sheepishly.

"Alright then. Off with you." His father said with a slight smile. Miles nodded his acknowledgement, leaned over kissing his mom's cheek and squeezing her shoulder. Then he strode out of his father's office and back out to his car.

Mary Beth stood up and walked around the desk to her husband's side, and he put his arm around her pulling her down onto his lap. She gazed into his eyes and stated sweetly, "If you don't give him the Café, I will buy it myself and give it to him. You and I both know he deserves to have it." She leaned in and kissed the tip of his nose.

"My two emotional hot heads. I love you both dearly." He said with a broad smile.

"Tommy...?"

"My love, as if I could resist you or your request." Thomas kissed her passionately. She always has been and would be his one weakness. He may be a wealthy powerful business man to the outside world, but with her he could truly be himself and let his guard down. He relied on her wisdom and counsel more that people realized and he did not intimidate her one iota. She held her own with him, and he loved that about her. She seemed cool, calm and collected but underneath was feisty and would fight for what she loved or believed in.

"As for Miles, I only wanted to see how badly he wanted it and that this was not just a day job to him. His temperament is so much like yours my dear, so easy going and affable, but for a man, I had to know he was going to be willing to fight for it. Otherwise it's not worth having and would ultimately fail, thus destroying his self-esteem. I have felt like he has been at this place for the last four months, but he had to want it enough to ask for it. I don't worry about that with Sebastian, he is driven and aggressive so I pretty much know where he stands on everything. After seeing how Miles handled Candace last week, and the counsel he gave her, he has matured so much. Sebastian would have never gotten that far with her and most likely would have sent her spiraling out of control. We made the right choice in sending Miles."

"I love you Thomas Petersen," she said laying her head on his chest.

"You are my heart." He said wrapping his arms around her.

Chapter 9

Damages

The week for Miles seemed to be one endless day that rolled into the next. The only exciting thing this week was that they started training Candy at the Café. Surprisingly the staff seemed energetic and encouraging where she was concerned. Although she had a tendency to whine a little, she did pretty well, getting up early and getting on a scheduled much to Miles's surprise. They were limiting her duties to the cash register, serving, and cleanup for now and the espresso machines were off limits; Katie had made that quite clear. Things were so far so good, and since Candy had the gift of gab the clients seemed to enjoy her and she was making good tips.

Ava's week was going by quickly, the trade show started off slowly but after the first day she had remained steady. Not only was she able to do some networking with other vendors, but was also selling quite a bit of product. Next year she may have to hire someone to watch the store, so she and Maggie both come to the trade show. She really could have used an extra hand. Thankfully at night she was so tired that she just crashed in the room and went to bed early. By Thursday, she was ready for the weekend, and much to her amazement ready to see Miles. She felt empty inside she missed him so much.

With the threat of in climate weather approaching, the trade show disbanded early so the vendors and guests could get back home safely. Ava was grateful, and since she had sold almost all of her wares, she had very little to pack. She got on the road fairly quickly and made it back to Mapleton right as the weather turned for the worse. Town was located much further north of Charlotte, and it had apparently been snowing here for hours. They had at least five inches so far, and in hind sight she realized she should have left Charlotte much earlier.

Ava knew she had nothing to eat at her house, so decided to run into the grocery store at the edge of town to pick up some essentials. She entered quickly as they were getting ready to close, and in a small hand basket gathered some bread, fruit, juice, soup and some crackers. She made her way to a check out register and was probably fourth in line to check out when she heard someone call her name. She looked over and saw Miles with a tall blonde hanging on his arm, leaning into him laughing and talking. *I can't believe it! Is he with that girl from the Hollywood movie crew that was in the Café the other day? He's headed this way! Is he serious?*

All at once, she felt a sharp pain in her chest, everything started spinning. She had to get out of there and now! She dropped her basket where she stood then ran out the door to her car. It was sleeting now and hot tears ran down her cheeks as she started the car and took off out of the parking lot.

Miles came back into the estate in a fury. He entered the kitchen, slammed the groceries down and slung his keys across the counter top. They came to an abrupt stop when they hit the dark gray granite backsplash. He stood bracing himself against the cool granite counter top his head hung low and his hair fell framing his face.

"How could I have been so irresponsible?" He snarled at no one in particular. Candy had walked in cautiously behind him trying to give him a wide berth. She had never seen him react that way before, and frankly it frightened her. The Miles she knew was good natured and calm, always finding the silver lining in the storm. He was so angry in the car on the ride home, barely speaking a word, he just kept staring at his cell phone as though he could will it to ring.

"Miles, you are being too hard on yourself. We are like family, and you had no way of knowing she would be at *that* grocery store. You called her, right? Give her some time and I'm sure she will call you back." With that she gave him a sympathetic look and walked out of the kitchen and headed into the den with the rest of the family.

Taking off his gloves, and jacket then tossing it over the back of the bar stool, Miles was pacing back and forth in the kitchen running his hands through his hair and looking down at the phone on the counter top.

"Ava, please call. Please Ava." He repeated over and over. He was so excited when he saw her in the grocery store that he made a bee line straight for her, oblivious to the fact he still had Candy laughing and pulling on his arm. Ava turned and momentarily their eyes locked. The look on her face was gut wrenching. Her pale delicate features literally crumbled when she saw him with Candy hanging all over him and her usually vivid blue eyes filled with tears. She dropped her small basket of items and ran from the store out into the wintery mix. He kept torturing himself, reliving this scene over and over in his mind.

Completely lost in his thoughts, he did not hear his mother enter the kitchen and turned abruptly nearly knocking her over. He reached out quickly and steadied her with his strong firm hands.

"Oh mother, I'm sorry. I didn't hear you come in." He exclaimed sounding exasperated.

She reached up with both hands and cupped his face, Miles leaned into her hand and stood there and closed his eyes. Mary Beth knew he was worried and that he had been struggling with something serious over the past few weeks but he was reluctant to share, she thought perhaps it was the Café and the conversation with his dad, but that went well. Obviously there was something else.

"My sweet son. It pains me to see you so distressed. I wish I could fix this for you." He reached up and took her hands in his, then kissed the back of her hand.

"I wish you could too mom. I've been praying, seeking answers but God has been silent."

A whirring sound interrupted his train of thought as he realized his phone was vibrating against the countertop and the picture on the caller id showed Ava's face. Miles spun around to grab the phone, his face reflected relief as he looked back at his mom. Ava had called! It was a step in the right direction, even if she was angry, at least she had called back.

"Ava? Thank God." His voice pitched in anticipation. Her voice on the other end was faint, but he heard her say "Miles?" She sounded confused. He pressed the phone closer to his ear.

"Yes, oh Ava I am so happy you called…"

"shhhhh. Miles. I …. am…in….trouble." She sound all wrong her voice was strained, and winded. His face fell and he motioned for his mother to stay close by.

"What's wrong? Are you ok? " He tried his best to remain calm and sound in control, but his insides betrayed him.

"Car …..crash…...I'm hurt Miles ….but I have to tell you I …..love…..you. It's always been….you." Her voice but a whisper.

"Ava, I love you so much. Where are you? Please tell me, and I'll come get you." He pleaded but there was silence.

"Ava I can't live without you, please tell me where you are." The emotion in his voice was raw.

"It's ok Miles. You don't have to say ….it….back….. I know it was ….just business to you…" her voice trailed off. She was starting to shake uncontrollably now. The cold had soaked through her clothes and now into her bones.

"Business? No Ava! Why would you say that?"

"Miles I'm scared……and I'm so cold….please help me….." her voice even softer now and quivering. Miles was pacing the kitchen in a full blown panic, pressing the phone even harder against his ear in an effort to hear her soft words. His mother just stood back watching helplessly as her youngest son was having one of the toughest conversations of his life, and there was nothing she could do.

"Ava, please tell me where you are, honey please, you're scaring me. I need to know where you are." His voice cracked.

By this time his father and Sebastian had entered the kitchen, listening and watching him pace frantically trying to keep her on the phone. His mother whispered "He's talking to Ava, but something is terribly wrong." They all stood anxiously waiting to hear what would be said next. His mother's eyes bored into her eldest son, and he looked guilty. Sebastian stood ready to do whatever was needed. He could not help but feel that he was at the very least partially responsible for this situation and the gravity of it was crushing his chest. Watching his younger brother in so much distress, was heartbreaking. Even for him.

"one, nine, six, bridge." is all she could manage.

"You are at the bridge on Highway 196?"

With that information Sebastian whipped out his cell phone and called 911 alerting them to an accident on the Highway 196 Bridge. Now he began pacing opposite Miles working off his own nervous energy as he quietly spoke to the operator.

"Miles...you there......?" Ava said almost unintelligibly.

"Yes, yes baby I'm here, I'm going to come get you. Hang on Ava, I'm coming." He said desperately trying to find the keys he had thrown earlier.

"No time.... Miles....I'm so cold........." her words came slow and deliberate. He could tell it was taking all her energy just to keep talking to him, but he was unwilling to let her off the phone.

"Ava, I'm coming right now, I can be there in a few minutes. Stay with me Ava, please stay with me." He pleaded with her.

"Tell Maggie...." A faint whisper escaped her.

He realized she was slipping away, that he was losing her. He was livid to find himself in this situation and his voice became desperate "No! No Ava. You can tell her yourself. You have to hang on for me, I'm on my way." He located his keys and held them tightly in his fist. His voice softened again, "Ava?"

"Miles......pray...." She was barely audible now, then silence. It was an eerie silence and Miles literally slid down the cabinets until he landed on the floor, his knees drawn up and the phone still pressed tightly to his ear.

"Ava? Are you still with me honey?" His voice now soft and tentative. Tears now starting to fall down his cheeks.

"Ava.....please...are you there?" he pleaded his voice hoarse now. "No!!!!!!!!!" he cried out as his head hung low and the tears now were freely flowing.

She was gone. His family stood there horrified, not believing what had just taken place. After a minute of complete silence, Sebastian burst forward. He grabbed Miles by the shoulders and commanded "Miles, let's go! Now! Get up, let's go! I'll drive you, give me the keys."

Miles just sat there motionless, his will to move paralyzed by grief and the words that Sebastian spoke were not registering.

"Come on! Miles…we can do this. Let's go find her." Once again he tugged at Miles's arm, this time Miles looked up at him pitifully with eyes rimmed in red and tear streaked cheeks. "Yeah that's it brother, get up and we'll go find her." he said reassuringly.

"Sebastian…" his mother started, with a look of caution. He looked over at her and nodded "Mom, I've got this. I swear I will take care of him." He half smiled and then focused his attention back on his younger brother.

His father stepped in to help Sebastian get him up and moving towards the garage, he grabbed his jacket and gloves. Miles legs felt like lead and his feet did not want to cooperate. He stumbled out of the kitchen into the garage still holding the phone to his ear, dazed. They managed to get him in the Land Rover and Sebastian got in on the driver's side, he turned back towards his mother and blew her a kiss. Their mother stood back in the door way watching her two beloved children drive off into near blizzard like conditions. She understood that one way or another they had to go, Sebastian seemed to need this as much as Miles did.

She was unsure of what was really going on between those two but it had been years since she had seen Sebastian show any real compassion for his brother. Perhaps something worthy would come out of this tragedy? Thomas came to his wife's side and she broke down in tears. He had never felt so helpless in his entire life. He walked her back inside to the warmth of the house, and filled the Weston's in on what had taken place. Candace took it especially hard and started wailing upon hearing of Ava's death. She felt responsible for the whole grocery store incident and was inconsolable. They all gathered at Thomas's request and held hands and started praying for Ava, Miles and Sebastian.

Sebastian drove towards the bridge as fast as he could without killing them both in the process. He turned on the four wheel drive option on the Land Rover and that helped as much as anything for traction in the snow. Miles sat with his head against the side glass window and was murmuring, tears still streaming down his face. Sebastian surmised he was praying, which caused him to lift up some silent pleas of his own. *Dear God if you can hear me, please forgive me for what I have done. I've destroyed two lives and I don't know what to do. For the first time in my life I am afraid and so ashamed. Please help Miles God…..please!*

Sebastian's phone started ringing and he fumbled in his pocket finally pulling it out. He didn't recognize the number but answered it anyway.

"Petersen here."

"This is the Mountain County sheriff's department, did you report an accident on Highway 196 at the Bridge?"

"Yes, yes I did."

"Hold one moment for the officer at the scene. Roger 2-76 go ahead." the dispatcher relayed.

"Yes this is Officer Miller, who am I speaking with please?"

"Sebastian Petersen. We believe my brother's girlfriend was involved in an accident there."

"We found a female approximately twenty five years old. Her vehicle went off the bridge and into the river."

"Oh my God." Sebastian slowed the car and pulled over. There were no other cars on the road in this mess and he sat there stunned to think of her demise. He desperately wished he could trade places with her, he would do anything right now to spare his brother from this nightmare.

"We are transporting her to Mercy General, they have a trauma team there on standby. I wanted to let you know, so that you would not waste time going into the city. Apparently there is a visiting trauma surgeon that got trapped by the weather and is stuck at Mercy. He's scrubbing and waiting on her to arrive."

"Are you telling me she is alive? We thought….."

"Yes, but the situation is very touch and go right now, so there is no time to lose, she is bleeding internally. If you know her family you need to call them in."

"We were on our way to the bridge, but I am turning around now and heading for the hospital. Thank you for calling."

"Miles, we are going to the hospital, that's where they are taking Ava. Miles she's alive! She is very sick buddy, but she's alive. Miles do you hear me?" Sebastian said trying to get a reaction from Miles, who was suffering from shock.

"Ok." He said softly.

Sebastian turned then headed to the hospital, the ambulance was just ahead of them by about four minutes. He grabbed Miles's phone and scrolled down until he found Natasha's number.

"Hello? Miles?" She answered.

"Please don't hang up, it's important. It's Sebastian." He said almost breathless.

"What's wrong? You are scaring me."

"I need to get in touch with Ava's friend. The gal with curly hair. Mandy or"

"Maggie" she cut him off. "Why?"

"Ava has been in a horrible accident and is being taken to Mercy General here in town."

"No! Take her to the city. Oh my God was Miles with her?"

"No, he was on the phone with her though. It was horrible. Listen there is a specialist at Mercy, they have her now. Please get her friend there. It's serious. Thank you Natasha, and I'm sorry. I'm sorry about everything." With that he hung up.

Natasha felt ill, she searched her phone for Maggie's number. She relayed the message and Maggie left right then to head to the hospital. She hoped she would be able to make it in time with the weather being so horrible.

Sebastian helped get Miles out of the car, and the cold air seemed to breathe a little life back in him. As they were walking through the snow up towards the hospital entrance, Sebastian had a crisis of conscience turning to Miles, "Listen, I have to tell you something brother. Please I have to say this to you now."

Miles paused and just looked at him expressionless. "It's all my fault. Everything. Miles I am so so sorry. I told Ava that you used her to get information for the space and that you didn't love her. I would do anything to take it back and make it right, I swear. I was jealous and nasty. I would not blame you if you hated me forever." Sebastian now breathless, stood there shivering looking at Miles waiting for his reaction.

Miles stepped forward slowly with a completely blank look on his face, he got about two feet from his brother and threw a punch that landed squarely in Sebastian's face sending him reeling backwards, Miles slipped in the snow landing on his knees.

"Why?" He screamed at Sebastian. "Why do you hate me so much? You have everything Sebastian! Everything! Father's attention, the business, money, and all I ever wanted was the Café and Ava! Now you have taken that from me." Miles's shoulders hunched over and his now wet hair hung in his face, as he knelt there in the snow sobbing. Sebastian recovered from the hit, but made no attempt to defend himself against Miles. He welcomed it, and wished that Miles would hit him again. He knew he deserved that and more if would help serve his penance, he was willing to endure it.

"I was stupid and jealous! I never expected any of this.....Miles I swear to you I will spend the rest of my life making this up to you. Although my actions as of late speak differently, I do love you Miles, you are my brother." He said desperately.

Miles stood up slowly breathing heavily, and wiped his face with his hands, verses rushing to his mind and then once again moved towards Sebastian who braced himself for another blow. A blow that never came.

Miles stuck his hand out slowly as if he were going to shake Sebastian's hand. Tentatively, Sebastian reached out and Miles grabbed his hand pulling him in tight for a hug and then whispered in his ear. "I forgive you." He slowly released Sebastian's hand then turned away from him to walk inside. Sebastian stood there shivering in the snow with tears now streaming down his face.

Miles found the emergency room attendant and told them he was there for Ava Turner, his fiancée who had been in an accident. They directed him to the family waiting area, and informed him that she was in surgery. They would update him as they received information. The nurse that led him to the waiting area noticed he was soaking wet and came back with a blanket for him. He sat in there alone, with his head in his hands. His hand was killing him and his head hurt, but he was praying and thanking God for sparing his Ava.

Maggie drove up and parked in the first space she could find which was in the handicapped area closest to the door and started inside. She noticed a man standing outside visibly shaken and as she got closer she saw it was Sebastian. She approached him cautiously and saw he had been crying. He looked up and their eyes met. He spoke first, "Maggie, please forgive me. This is all my fault. I said things to upset Ava and caused the problems between her and Miles. I am so sorry. Truly I am so sorry."

She walked over and punched him in the stomach. Screaming, "How could you? You are a terrible person!" As soon as she said the words out loud, she regretted them. Upon closer inspection it looked as though Miles might have taken a swing at him too. She left him standing there in the snow slightly hunched over and wet.

Maggie found her way to the family waiting area, and saw a shattered looking Miles. Running to him and throwing her arms around him then breaking down into tears. They sat there together clinging to one another, neither one speaking. There were no words right now, just two friends holding each other and silently praying for their mutual love.

Sebastian also found his way into the hospital and asked where the chapel was located. He made his way down the hallway, self-conscience at the noise his shoes made on the floor as he walked. He entered in the small empty chapel and welcomed the soothing music that was playing lightly in the background. Sebastian fell at the small alter and once again poured his heart out to God. Begging for forgiveness, praying for Ava, and for Miles. He felt so ashamed and small.

About an hour and a half later, the nurse announced that the surgery was complete and Ava was in recovery, she would be placed in the I.C.U. She stated the doctor would be in shortly to see them and explain everything, so they both stood there and just held each other. The doctor came in and explained her injuries, she suffered a concussion, left arm was broken, and a collapsed lung due to broken rib puncture. Some internal organ damage with internal bleeding that they think they have stopped for now. She was still in a lot of danger and the next 36 hours were crucial. He informed them he was spending the night at the hospital and would be there if anything went wrong. Miles stepped up and thanked him for saving Ava's life and praised God for the snow that kept him stranded here in Mapleton for the night. The doctor smiled and patted him on the back. "Amen son. Amen."

Maggie looked up at Miles, "Where's Sebastian?"

"Ah I don't know. Maybe in the main waiting area?"

"The nurse is going to take you to see Ava, I'll go and find him."

"Maggie, please don't be too hard on him. He's hurting too. I know he may seem sub-human to you right now, but he is still my brother. So for me?"

"I got this Miles. Go see our girl. I'll be up in a bit." She said with a reassuring smile.

Maggie walked out into the main waiting area and looked around but no sign of Sebastian. She stopped at the nurse's station and described him. A cute petite attendant stated she saw a man fitting that description headed towards the chapel. She thanked her and headed that way, she knew this hospital like the back of her hand since she volunteered here. She entered the chapel quietly and saw him sitting all alone on the first pew with his head down and shoulders rounded. Maggie was overcome with emotion seeing him broken like that, she walked softly then sat down next to him and put her hand over his. He never looked up but took her hand and put it between his two. Sebastian's hands were warm and soft and they both just sat for a few minutes in silence.

"Ava is out of surgery and Miles is in I.C.U. with her right now." She said softly. She heard his voice catch as he tried to speak and then he paused to regain his composure.

"Thank you. Thank you for letting me know. I'm very sorry for everything Maggie."

"I know you are." She said kindly. "How is your face?"

"It hurts, but I deserve the pain."

"I should probably apologize for punching you, but I was angry. Very angry."

"Please don't."

"Well, I'm just saying, it's not very lady like." Maggie stated with a slight grin and nudged him with her shoulder. Which got a small smile out of him. "Oh don't make me smile…. now that really smarts."

"Come on, I'll buy you a coffee or get you an ice pack or something." She said, her hand still tucked away inside of his.

"An Advil and an ice pack sound great about now, but I'll settle for a coffee. However, I must insist on buying you one."

"Suit yourself, but just know I don't come cheap. You've been warned. I may even get a sweet roll."

Now it was his turn to grin and bump her with his shoulder. "Deal."

They were interrupted by the sound of his phone buzzing. Answering, he quickly filled his father in on what had happened and that Ava was alive. He stated that it would take an army to remove Miles from her side and that more than likely he would drive Maggie home to ensure her safety and after that he would be home. He would bring Miles a change of clothes in the morning. He could hear the elation in his mother's voice when his father relayed the news that Ava had survived.

He ended the call, then he walked Maggie to the cafeteria for that coffee.

CHAPTER 10

Mercy

Miles sat as close to the bed as he could get without climbing in there with her. Ava looked swollen and there were tubes and blinking-beeping machines everywhere. To him she was beautiful, and the fact that she was even alive was nothing less than a miracle. He held her delicate small hand and kissed it tenderly. After thanking God repeatedly for sparing her, he prayed for her healing. He spoke softly to her in case she could hear him and reassured her that he was there, and that she was going to be ok.

Sebastian and Maggie stopped by I.C.U. after getting a coffee and Miles stepped out for a moment so Maggie could go in. He joined his brother in the hallway, and noticed the bruising was starting to settle around Sebastian's eye and Miles winced at the thought of what he had done.

"Get some ice on that when you get home." Miles said.

"Yeah, I'm fine. Are you gonna be ok?"

"She is alive, so I will be fine." He looked into Sebastian's eyes and for the first time in a long time he felt like he had his brother back.

"It's so late, I'm going to drive Maggie home, since we don't want any more accidents in this weather. I'll come back tomorrow to bring you a change of clothes and bring her back up to get her car. Can I get you anything before we leave?"

"No, I'm good thanks, a nurse brought me a Coke earlier. I'm not hungry right now but if I do get hungry I'll go downstairs. Has anyone called Ava's parents?"

"I will get with Maggie and we will notify them. Don't worry. Also, I am having them send her hospital bills to me. Whatever her insurance doesn't cover I will take care of for her. I don't want her to worry about this." Sebastian offered sincerely.

Miles put his hand on his brother's shoulder and squeezed it. Maggie came out giving Miles a hug then he went back in to sit at Ava's side. She and Sebastian moved quietly through the I.C.U. hallway, then he walked her to her car so she could move it out of the handicapped area. He pulled up in Miles's Rover and they headed towards her apartment. They drove in silence for a few minutes then Maggie exclaimed "Oh no! I've got to get in touch with Ava's parents. In all this excitement I totally forgot about them, but I bet they are snowed in too. They moved to Wisconsin about two years ago for her father's new job, so I'll have to find their information once I get to the house."

"Do you want me to stay with you while you speak to them?" He offered.

"I don't know, maybe? I know them really well, which is going to make it harder to tell them. What should I say?" She asked as her thoughts drifted.

"If I may, I would tell them she was in a car accident, but was treated by a terrific visiting surgeon, and is currently in I.C.U. in an abundance of caution. They expect a full recovery. Then mention the lesser injuries like her concussion and broken arm. People tend to focus on the last words they hear not the first. Then of course let them know we are all here and will stay with her until they can arrive safely. I know the airports near us have cancelled most of their flights, and driving would be treacherous too at this point."

"Ok, that sounds good. Thanks. Maybe I will have you stay if you don't mind, to help keep me focused. I tend to talk to fast and ramble sometimes." She smiled.

They pulled into her apartment complex and he was thankful she was on the ground floor, no icy stairs to traverse. She unlocked the door and they walked into her living room. He noticed that for someone who had such a vivid personality that her furnishings were quite tailored and traditional. Her space was tidy and welcoming. He sat on the sofa while she rummaged through a desk drawer to find her address book and just soaked in her surroundings.

She found their number and made the call holding Sebastian's hand while she spoke to them and he encouraged her as she tried to explain simply what had happened. They were of course distressed, but were comforted that she was surrounded by so many people who loved her. They would try to get a flight closer in to Mapleton and then drive the rest of the way. Maggie promised to keep them updated every couple of hours.

After hanging up the phone she exhaled and then released Sebastian's hand. He winked at her then stood and stated that he would come back for her in the morning to take her back to get her car. They had a total of about eight inches of snow so far, and the forecast was calling for another front to roll through later Saturday. Maggie was certainly seeing a different side of Sebastian and observed that he could really be a thoughtful, caring person. Which of course was a completely different impression than the one she previously had of him.

"Thank you for the coffee and the ride home. I appreciate you staying while I called the Turner's. So I'll see you in the morning?"

"Yes. Here is my business card, it has all of my information on it. I'll give you a call before I head over, if that is ok?"

"Sure, you have my number right?"

"Yes. Yes I do." He said flashing a Petersen smile, and with that he left her standing in the doorway as the tiny snowflakes continued to fall. She looked down at her watch and saw it was two a.m., she closed and locked the door. Kicking off her shoes and crawling into bed, she ended up sleeping in her clothes.

Sebastian drove back to the estate, and his father met him at the door. His mother and the Weston's had gone to bed after they learned Ava was alive, out of surgery and in I.C.U. After getting and ice pack for his eye area, they walked back to his father's office and his dad poured them a drink. Sebastian disclosed the entire ugly story to his father, and they spoke for a couple hours. Actually Thomas just listened allowing Sebastian to confess and get it all off his chest.

Thomas did finally give him some words of encouragement, and suggested Sebastian take a few weeks off from work. It was time their family was restored, and any issues resolved. Sebastian shuffled into his old bedroom exhausted, flopped across the bed, and he too slept in his clothes.

Miles stayed close to Ava laying his head down on her bed and sleeping off and on as he held her hand. The nurses were in and out every fifteen minutes it seemed. During the night the E.M.S. crew who had brought her to the hospital, came by to see how she was doing. Miles stepping out into the hall spoke thanking them for saving her. They indicated she was probably driving a little too fast for conditions, and that some kids were out sledding near the bridge. They feel like a group slid out in front of her and she over corrected to keep from hitting them. Her SUV hit the concrete railing then landed precariously up on it, teetering. Amazingly, she managed to get her seatbelt off and open her door then dropping to the sidewalk on the bridge, and that is most likely how she broke her left arm. Soon after she exited the vehicle, it tilted over the railing and fell into the icy river. She was incredibly lucky.

Miles was horrified to hear the events of what actually happened, and yet so grateful that she was not stranded in that vehicle. He shuddered to think of what could have happened. Thank God she got out. He was the last person to call her on her phone so when she tapped the screen it automatically redialed him and that is how she was able to call him. She had passed out due to the cold and severe pain she was in, and it was essential that Sebastian had made the call to 911 when he did. She would not have lasted out there much longer in those conditions.

Ava was quiet through the night and her vitals remained steady which was a huge victory. The visiting surgeon, came and checked on her about six a.m. He was pleased with her progress but stated they were not out of the woods yet. Another 24 hours would let us know if she was going to come out of this with a full recovery or not.

Sebastian woke around seven a.m. and pulled himself out of bed, stumbling into the shower. The hot water was a welcome treat, after being so wet and cold last night. His face felt tight where Miles had punch him and he knew it was going to be bruised. Still it was minor in comparison to what Ava was enduring right now and that was humbling, an emotion he did not spend much time in. He dressed warmly and made his way into the kitchen where he found his mom sitting, along with a pot of coffee she had made. She gasped when he rounded the corner getting a full shot of his face.

"Oh Sebastian! Honey what happened?" She said getting up touching his wounded face. Which caused him to wince a little.

"Mom, I'm fine really. You should see the other guy." He tried to joke, but he saw she was not buying it.

"Did Miles do that to you?"

"Mom, I assure you I deserved this and far more than what I got."

"It breaks my heart to see you two fighting. Especially when it gets physical." She said tearing up.

"Mother, Miles was provoked, he was hurting and in so much pain....Astonishingly it was him who showed me mercy, after everything I had put him through. I don't deserve him as a brother." He said quite contrite.

She reached up pulling him in close and hugged him. He laid his head on her shoulder and just held onto her. "Sebastian, you are a good man, you have a good heart. I want you to listen to that little voice in your head more. Take a chance honey and open up to people, let them see how wonderful you are. Promise me you will try." She whispered to him. All he could manage was a nod and squeezed her tightly.

Soon Candace and Melissa ambled into the kitchen, the aroma of coffee had wafted down the hall and woke them up. They too noticed his blacked eye but did not bring it up and Sebastian for one was grateful for their show of good manners. They chatted briefly about the weather and then of course asked about Ava. He filled them in on what he knew, and stated that Miles had texted him at some point early this morning and said she did well through the night.

His mother quietly reappeared with a small duffle bag for Miles, with two changes of clothes, and toiletry essentials. She also packed some snacks, phone charger and his iPod. "Sebastian, when you go, please take this to Miles he will need this."

"Yes ma'am, of course."

"Sebastian, I want to go see her. Will you wait while I get dressed really quick?" Candace piped up.

"Hurry, I need to pick up Maggie as well." He excused himself stepping into the living room where it was quiet to call Maggie. His call woke her up but she promised to be ready in five. He chuckled to himself and didn't doubt for a second that she could get ready in five minutes flat. He also called Natasha to fill her in on everything, telling her not to worry about trying to open the Café today. Just to enjoy her weekend and he would see her on Monday.

Remarkably by the time he reentered the kitchen after placing his phone calls, Candy was fully dressed, hair tied back in a neat bun, and ready to go.

As they got into the Rover, he made her sit in the backseat so that Maggie could sit up front, she protested slightly but did as he requested. She could be sulky at times and he was happy she did not pick this morning to start up. He was halfway to Maggie's front door when it flew open and there she stood in jeans, a red sweater with a white turtleneck underneath and a multicolored knit scarf around her neck. Her hair was tousled and she had a small barrette on the side holding her curly bangs out of her face. She had on simple earrings and a silver flower ring on her right hand. *Ready in five? You look amazing*, he thought to himself.

She grabbed her coat, gloves then turned and locked the door. As she got in the Rover Sebastian introduced her to Candace, explaining she was more like a little sister than a family friend. Both women smiled and shook hands. The hospital parking lot was fuller than they expected, so he dropped them off at the door then drove around to the side to park. They all walked up to I.C.U. together, a sterile smell greeted them as they exited the elevator, and made their way around to Ava's room. Miles had drifted off to sleep again, but stirred when he heard the curtain being pulled back. He stood slowly, kissed her hand, and then walked out to see everyone. The nurse made a beeline to check on Ava since he had moved from her side.

"Mom packed you a care bag." Sebastian said handing the duffle bag over. Miles smiled as he grabbed it.

"Oh Miles, you look horrible sweetie. Bless your heart, did you sleep at all?" Maggie said walking over and giving him a sideways hug. Miles just grinned, he could always count on Maggie to keep it real. Next Candace slowly walked over and then launched herself at Miles giving him a full body hug. Sebastian quickly put his hand to Miles's back to steady him, since she nearly knocked him over.

"Ok. Ok, Candy, I'm happy to see you too." Hugging her back with his one free arm.

"Let's get you some breakfast Miles. They are serving downstairs and it actually smelled really decent for hospital food. You need to eat something, since I'm sure you haven't eaten since early yesterday." Sebastian encouraged.

"I'll sit with her while you go, she'll be fine. I'll call if she like moves or anything." Candy offered. Miles grinned at Sebastian, she really did mean well.

"Ok, you guys win. I think I am a little hungry." He conceded.

They all watched as Candy sat next to the bed, and very gently touched Ava's hand with her finger. Candy stared at her intently with her phone in the other hand and ready to call if she so much as quivered. They went through the line in the cafeteria and the breakfast spread was actually quite decent. Bacon, sausage links, hash browns, scrambled eggs, or a veggie omelet, biscuits and gravy, assorted fruits and yogurts. Miles literally selected one of everything, and a large sweet tea. Sebastian selected an omelet, toast and a coffee, then Maggie picked up some fruit and a yogurt. Miles offered up grace and then proceeded to inhale his breakfast. He finished before the other two and went back for seconds. Clearly all this turmoil had turned up his appetite, and he was in need of the nourishment. Miles stopped to refill his tea once more before they headed back upstairs to the I.C.U.

Maggie had gone ahead of them and made arrangements with the head I.C.U. nurse to let Miles take a shower up there. They used to work together and she was more than happy to help her old friend out. Miles stopped by to see Ava first and then quickly made his way to the showers. He stepped out feeling refreshed and was thankful to have a change of clothes. They found a bag to put his dirty clothes in and Candace offered to wash all of it for him when she got home.

He went back in the room then took his place next to her side and thanked everyone for coming up. Maggie offered to stay there with him for a while so Sebastian gathered Candy and they went back to the house. Honestly, Sebastian was exhausted with only three hours of sleep and the emotional ordeal he had been through in the last twenty four hours. Candy talked non-stop on the way home and thankfully he had to do little more than nod to remain in the conversation.

They updated everyone when they arrived home, then Sebastian quietly snuck away to the stillness of his room and laid back down. Sleep overcame him and he did not resist it, the kind of rest he needed was long overdue. The Petersen house was quiet and peaceful today much like the white snow that lay outside....

Miles sat listening to the rhythmic beeps of the machines that kept him company while he watched over his sweet Ava as she was sleeping. He sent Maggie home about an hour before so that she could make it home before dark. He enjoyed her company for the afternoon. He kept talking to Ava, filling her in on everything that had gone on in the last week or so. He was aware that she probably couldn't hear anything he was saying, but it made him feel better to share with her what was on his mind. He missed their chats, he missed her.

A doctor stepped in and asked Miles to please step outside for a few minutes while they examined her. He was reluctant but did as he was asked. Her vitals had seemed steady all day and Miles took that as a sign she was going to make a full recovery. A nurse came alongside him then walked him down the hallway, he got the impression they did not want him near Ava right now and that alarmed him.

"What's going on? What are they doing to her?"

"They feel like she is doing well enough to remove the breathing tube. If you aren't used to seeing them removed, it can be disconcerting. They know you are already upset and I suggested we not traumatize you anymore than you already are."

"Thanks. So they think she can breathe on her own? That's a good sign right?"

"Yes. She may drop off initially, but then they are hoping she will hold her own."

"Maybe I should go get something to eat?"

"Yes, I have your number and will text you if there are any changes. Go stretch, walk around and get some dinner."

"Ok, I'll see you in thirty minutes." He promised.

Miles took the elevator down to the first floor and then turned towards the cafeteria. There were a couple of orderlies, a few doctors or med students, and one couple that sat in a corner by themselves. He ordered a six inch sub sandwich with pasta salad and a fruit cup. He sat at a table near the television with the weather on a scrolling loop. The next wave of the winter storm was almost upon them. *Great. More snow, that's what we need alright.*

He decided to call his parents, his mother answered so he filled her in on the day's activity. She of course expressed concern over him and Ava. Miles said to give everyone his love and he would call if there were any changes. He finished the last of his fruit cup and had to smile because it reminded him of being back in grade school. Some things never change. He picked up his tray then threw away his trash and hit the hand sanitizer on his way out the door.

Before heading back upstairs he stepped outside to see the weather first hand. It felt slightly warmer than it did last night by a degree or two and the wind had died down. He stood just looking up at the sky noticing there were a few breaks in the clouds allowing him to see a star or two, but the front was definitely on its way. Back in I.C.U. he stopped at the nurse's station to check and see if it was ok to go back in and sit with Ava. She assured him it was ok and Ava was fine. He made his way back to his love and sat by her side. The breathing tube was removed and replaced by a smaller nose piece that kept a steady stream of oxygen going to her lungs. Miles reached for her hand and gently traced his finger along her wrist and fingers. She stirred ever so slightly and her eyes fluttered.

"Nurse!" He exclaimed. Two of them came rushing in, one to his side, one checked the machines.

"What happened?" Nurse Jenny inquired.

"She stirred and her eyes fluttered. I thought she was waking up." He said startled.

"Ok, it's ok. She is going to wake up, it might be slow incoming, but she will. These are all good signs." She walked by and patted him on the arm.

"Sorry."

They smiled and went back to their station. He sat back down and began talking softly to her again. Exhaustion was creeping in and his bones felt weary. Once again he laid his head down near Ava's hand and threw his arm across her legs. He drifted off to sleep, and sometime later he woke to something stroking his cheek ever so lightly. He lifted his head up and saw that her eyes were barely open and her finger was moving trying to touch him.

"Ava?" He said softly. The corner of her mouth turned slightly upward. *A smile!* "Hi baby, I'm here. You are going to be ok."

"Mi....les" she tried.

"Shhh. Its ok, not sure you should try to speak just yet. You had a tube down your throat and it's probably really dry. Let me see if you can have some ice chips." His heart was pounding in his chest. *She's awake!*

He buzzed for the nurse who came in right away, and saw that Ava was awake. She checked her vitals and then sent Miles to the ice machine for a cup of shaved ice. He sprinted down the hall and was back before she could blink.

"Miles, give her very few at a time, she has been through a lot. Just set them on her tongue and let them melt. I'm going to alert the doctor."

Ava still was not fully awake even though her eyes were open, but he would take it. Feeding her ice chips was like watching a baby bird being fed. Her mouth was so dry and she yearned for the moisture. He tried to go slow like the nurse suggested but Ava's big blue eyes were pleading with him for more.

"I know baby, but you have to go slowly." As quickly as she started, she faded off and was out again. Miles sat back not sure what had just happened. He set the ice chips on the tray then went back to holding her hand and watching her. The doctor finally made it in to see her and was pleased with what he saw. He told Miles to be patient, it's only been twenty four hours since her surgery. A couple hours later her parents arrived to find him once again sleeping by her side.

The station nurse updated them on Ava's condition then filled them in on Miles. Nurse Jenny went in to wake Miles to let him know her parents had arrived and they wanted to see her. He walked out and introduced himself shaking Mr. Turner's hand, Mrs. Turner rushed past him to see her baby girl. Miles stayed behind and allowed Mr. Turner to go in and see her. He sat in the hallway across from the nurse's station not quite knowing what to do with himself now that the Turner's had arrived.

He texted Maggie, and was surprised when she texted him right back. It seemed like nobody was getting much sleep these days. He let her know that Ava's parents were in town and were in with her at the moment. Mr. Turner walked back out and sat next to Miles on the bench.

"Mr. Turner, you guys must be beat with all that traveling. Are you going on to Ava's tonight?"

"Please call me Rob, I'm not sure yet, her mother is reluctant to leave, but I could use a decent night's rest. So are you gonna head on home son? I know you must be exhausted, the nurse said you have barely left her side. I appreciate that."

"No sir. I have no plans to go home. If Mrs. Turner wants to stay, I'll just stay out here so she can have some privacy."

"Are you sure?"

"Yes, sir. I am fine. I love your daughter, and I want to be near her."

"I see. Well we have certainly heard a lot about you and it's nice to finally meet although the circumstances are regrettable. I'm just so relieved she is going to make a full recovery."

"Yes sir." Miles nodded.

"I think I'll go check on Anita." He patted Miles's knee and stood stretching his low back, then turned and walked towards Ava's room. After about ten minutes they both emerged from the room, stopped by briefly at the nurse's station and then came over to where Miles sat. He rose as Mr. Turner spoke and informed him that they were going to go on to the house to get a good night's sleep, then be back bright and early in the morning. Miles wished them well and said he would see them then. He waited until they were in the elevator before he turned and went back to Ava's side.

Her eyes fluttered open again around two a.m. Miles spoke softly to her and she seemed to understand what he was saying. He told her that her parents had arrived safely, they had been there, but were at her house resting until morning. He saw a small smile spread across her face and she seemed relieved.

"Ava, I love you so much. I always have. I don't want to overwhelm you with details, but Sebastian said things to you that weren't true to hurt me, and you. He has confessed and apologized profusely to me, but I know that it does not completely absolved him of the wrong he has caused. Please know that I have always loved you. I nearly died when I thought I had lost you in that accident." Miles held her hand and kissed it lightly.

Her big blue eyes let him know that she was taking all that in, and she squeezed his hand as hard as she was able. He brushed her hair gently off her forehead, and made sure she was warm enough under the blankets. She glanced over at the cup, and he realized she wanted more ice chips.

"I'll go get you some more ice chips, those have melted." He got up and quickly headed to the ice machine.

"Ok baby, we have to go slowly, ok?" Miles flashed her one of his amazing Petersen smiles.

Ava nodded ever so slightly, and she felt happy inside to learn that Miles did love her and that he was here by her side. She ached all over, and felt somewhat foggy but was awake and understood everything he said to her. Her arm felt like it weighed a ton, and she was having trouble moving it. Apparently she had been in an accident, the details of which she could not immediately recall.

Miles could see she was fidgeting a bit and so he informed her that her left arm was broken and in a cast. He saw her brow unfurrow and her shoulders relax. The nurse came back in to check on Ava so Miles stepped back outside to allow for privacy. When he returned back to her room she had fallen back asleep again. His heart was grieving as he wanted more time with her. He knew he would have to be patient, especially since her parents were here now, and they would want to be with her too.

Since she was resting, he went back through all the texts that he had received during the day. Word had gotten out and he was receiving texts from his staff, people at church and of course his family and Maggie. It was comforting to know so many people were lifting them up, more importantly her. Miles believed in the power of prayer and fully expected her to recover from these injuries.

He texted Sebastian asking him to please come back to the hospital in the morning once he was up and ready. That Ava's parents had arrived and he needed to come home and take care of a few things. He sat in the chair watching and waiting for her to open her eyes once more but she never did. He was not able to go back to sleep, and as promised the Turners were there at seven a.m. sharp. He filled them in on her night and her mother was elated she had woken up for a few minutes.

Thankfully Sebastian was not far behind them so Miles gathered his things. He told Nurse Jenny he would see her later. He told the Turner's he was going home to change and so forth, but would be back in the evening. Sebastian could see it was tearing Miles apart to leave her, but he knew Miles understood her parents needed time with their daughter. He grabbed Miles's duffle bag and carried it out for him. Miles got into the passenger's side of the Rover leaned back in the seat and closed his eyes.

"Thanks for coming Sebastian."

"Sure. I was surprised to get your text, but then when you said her parents were here… By the way mother and Melissa are fixing us breakfast."

"Ok." With that he closed his eyes until they pulled in at the estate. He looked disheveled and exhausted, when he entered the kitchen his mother and Melissa both pounced on him. He managed a weak smile and returned the hugs.

Breakfast was ready and although he was hungry he was having a hard time making it through the meal. Everyone noticed so they kept the chatter to a minimum. He finished and thanked them for breakfast, then Sebastian drove him the short distance to the guest cottage and left his Rover there. Sebastian walked back and got his vehicle and headed down to the Café. Miles took a quick shower and went straight to bed. Zelda found her way in and leaped on the bed and curled up right beside him; Miles never even stirred.

Chapter 11

New Beginnings

The weather was wretched outside and the roads were still covered in snow and ice. Tim picked up Natasha and Sammy had walked to work since he lived downtown. Sebastian wanted to hold a staff meeting so they pulled a couple of tables together so they could meet.

"I want to thank everyone for being here this morning. There is a lot going on, so I wanted to let you know what's happening and give you a chance to ask questions. As you may or may not know, Ava Turner was involved in a terrible car accident Friday night and nearly lost her life. Miles has been with her non-stop at the hospital, he is home now and resting but will return there again tonight."

"Is she going to be ok?" Sammy interrupted.

"Yes, she is expected to make a full recovery. I want to acknowledge that in the past I have acted atrociously and I do not expect to win your trust or respect by apologizing, but I hope in time that will come. I am very sorry for things I have said and done. I will be here temporarily helping to run things while Miles is tending to Ava and her recovery. Once she has fully recuperated, Miles will be taking over the Café permanently."

Everyone started clapping and smiling. Sebastian tried not to take it personally, he knew that they were just happy for Miles and all the hard work he had put into the Café. He knew Miles deserved to have the Café, and honestly was ready to let him have it.

"There's one more thing. We will be expanding into the next building space over the next few weeks. We are going to be sharing that space with La Noel, but I would like for that to remain a secret to surprise Miles and Ava. Well that's all I have, does anyone have anything they would like to say or have any questions?" He sat and waited a few minutes and no one spoke up.

"That's all for now, I'll try and stay out of your way, but please let me know if there is anything I can do for you. And if you need to talk privately, I'll be in the office. Thank you again." He stood and walked back to the office. *That went better than expected. Hopefully in time I can earn their trust.*

Natasha smiled at Tim, then they fist bumped each other and started cleaning up. It was time to make the house coffee blend, so Sammy went downstairs to get some supplies. They expected business would be light today with the roads still covered in snow. However, they did notice that the hardware store across the street was open for business, and the pharmacy was also open. Other than those two, the rest of the stores remained dark.

Sebastian picked up his cell phone to call Maggie. It went to voicemail and he asked her to please return his call that he had some business dealings he wanted to discuss with her. It was clear that Ava was going to be out of commission for a while and he wanted to offer Candace's services at the La Noel. Retail is her middle name and she would fare better there than the Café especially since they had just trained Sammy. Not to mention, Maggie was going to need a hand during their busy season. Plus he wanted to clue her in on the renovations to get her assistance and input on Ava's behalf.

Maggie took dinner up to the Turner's and insisted they eat something. Ava had been awake several times today and her family was very encouraged with her progress. She was sitting up and talking some, but still did not recall the events of the accident. The doctor said that it was most likely temporary and she may remember in time. Although she was elated to see her parents, she kept looking for Miles to walk in at any minute and he never came. Maggie knew that look and while Ava's folks took the basket of food to the cafeteria, she cozied up to her best friend and reassured her.

"I see that look on your face sweetie. I want you to know Miles has barely left your side since the accident, and it took everything in him to walk out that door and leave you so your parents could have some time alone with you. Please don't question his loyalty baby girl, he is crazy about you. I have seen it firsthand."

"I know, but I miss him." She said softly.

"Oh I would bet all my worldly possessions he'll be back tonight." She said grinning from ear to ear. Looking down at her phone she realized she had missed a call. Leaning over and kissing Ava on the cheek she excused herself to check her voicemail. *Sebastian wants me to call him? I wonder what's going on.* She pressed redial and he picked up on the third ring and sounded winded.

"Hello?"

"Hey Sebastian, Its Maggie, did I catch you in the middle of something?"

"Hello, Yes. Thank you for returning my call. Uh No. Sorry." He said trying to sound more composed.

"Which is it?" she said laughing at him.

"Yes I *was* in the middle of something, but well, I'm happy you returned my call. Are you available tonight by chance?"

"I don't know? Whatcha got in mind?"

"I just wanted to discuss a few business ideas with you, I would value your input."

"Wow, really? This is Maggie. Maggie Willis. Are you sure you called the right girl?" She said ribbing him.

"Yeah... I think I've got the right gal. If you are up for it?" He said smirking on the other end. *Boy this one was sassy,* and he liked that about her.

"Is there food involved? Because I am starving." She exclaimed.

"I'll see if I can find a sweet roll."

"Deal. I'll be home in an hour."

"An hour then."

She walked back into Ava's room but decided not to tell her it was Sebastian who had called. Best to see what he wants first. She didn't want to upset her friend in her delicate condition. Ava looked really tired, and Maggie encouraged her to get some rest. The Turner's returned and Maggie said her goodbyes and promised to come back tomorrow.

The drive home was slow going, the snow was still packed and icy patches made for a slippery ride. Maggie remembered half way home, that she had started a crockpot full of spaghetti, which sounded really good about now. She parked the car and pulled out her phone and texted Sebastian. *Dinner is made, come hungry. Mags*

Sebastian got the text as he was dropping Miles off at the hospital. Miles spoke very little in the car and acted as though he were sedated. He literally slept all day, and Candy had to literally shake him to wake him up at five thirty. He took a quick shower, changed, grabbed his backpack and met Sebastian in the garage.

"Call or text me when you want to come home." Sebastian called after him.

"Thanks." He nodded and went up the ramp that led to the hospital entrance.

Sebastian reached down and checked his phone and laughed at the text. *She is something alright. I have never met anyone like her before.*

Miles walked through the hallway at the hospital like he was in slow motion. He knew he was awake since he was upright and moving, but his head was foggy and his limbs felt heavy. He stepped off the elevator and made his way to Ava's room. Her father was at the nurse's station inquiring about ice chips.

"Mr. Turner, how is Ava today?"

"Miles!" He stuck out his hand for a shake. "Good, she is awake and even sat up today for a short time."

Miles nodded and a smile broke out across his face. "Mr. Turner, I'll get the ice chips then be right in."

"Avie, Miles is here, he is getting your ice chips." Her father said.

Ava perked up, and her mother took notice glanced at her father who was happy to see her face light up. Looking at his wife he gave her a knowing look. "I think we will head home for the night and get some rest, since the Calvary is here." Begrudgingly his wife kissed Ava's cheek and gathered her pocketbook.

Miles walked in and saw she had gathered her things and was a little perplexed. "Hi Mrs. Turner it's nice to see you again. I hope you guys aren't leaving on my account."

"No. No dear, we've been up since early this morning and we need to make some arrangements at the house. Were you able to get some rest today, you still look tired." Mrs. Turner replied.

"Yes ma'am I did, but I am still a little tired. I'll call you if there are any major changes of course. Get some rest and we'll see you in the morning?"

"Yes. Have a good night." She patted his arm as she went by, and Mr. Turner gave him a wink.

Ava was trying so hard not to fall back asleep, she wanted desperately to spend some time with Miles. She couldn't help but notice he looked terrible, dark circles still encompassed his eyes and his skin looked sallow. Even with all that he was a sight for her sore eyes and she reached out her hand for his.

"Hey sweetie.....I have missed you." He said trying to pull off a Petersen smile.

"Miles, you look exhausted. Did you rest at all?"

"Yeah I did, but I still feel kind of zonked." He tried to laugh. Taking her hand and dragging a chair closer to her he sat gazing into her big blue eyes.

"How are you today? How are you feeling?"

"Ok, not great, but ok. Pain has been off and on."

"You look tired baby. I'm here all night, why don't you get some rest?"

"Come closer and I will. I'm so happy you are here."

He brought the chair over closer and held her hand, he pushed the button that tilted the bed back slightly so she could get comfortable. Now he knew why he didn't rest well at home, the buzzing and whirring of the machines weren't there to keep him company. He watched as she closed her eyes and nestled under the covers to get comfortable. He folded his arms across his chest and slid back in the chair and tried to get settled. Nurse Tammy came in and brought an extra chair for him to prop his long legs up on. He smiled and thanked her.

Sebastian pulled up in front of Maggie's apartment and grabbed his jacket from the back seat. She was busy making the angel hair pasta to go with her meat sauce. Thankfully she had half a loaf of French bread left and made garlic bread which was toasting in the oven. The house smelled heavenly if she did say so herself. He rang the doorbell and within seconds she threw the door open and then bolted back to the kitchen. "Sorry!! Garlic bread in the oven, I don't want it to burn!" She called after him and asked him to come on inside.

"It smells wonderful. I'm amazed you could pull this together so quickly."

"Well when you called and asked me out or over or well... Anyway, I was caught off guard and forgot I had spaghetti in the crockpot. I hope you are not disappointed that we are not going out to eat."

"Spaghetti is one of my favorites. Thank you for inviting me."

"Oh. OH! The bread! Argg! Well I hope you like yours....toasty." She said a little embarrassed and exasperated as she removed it from the oven, it had gotten a little too brown.

"Actually I do. I prefer it crisp." He said flashing an amazing smile showing off his dimples and for the first time he looked like Miles to her.

"Aren't you the perfect guest? Well thank you for saying that, have a seat and we'll be plating up in just a minute."

He sat on the couch and noticed for the first time since entering her apartment that she had Dean Martin playing softly in the background. Again it made him smile, she was so eclectic and full of surprises.

"If you don't mind eating in here, I have a small dining area. Dinner is ready."

"No of course not, wherever you like. I'm starving."

"What would you like to drink? I have water, sprite and cranberry juice?"

"Any wine?"

"Uh No. I don't drink, but I do have some that I cook with, not sure how good it would be though."

"Water is fine. Thank you." he said taking a seat.

The small table had four chairs and a red table cloth with an old-time vino bottle candle holder with wax drippings as the centerpiece.

The kitchen was small but bigger than it appeared from the living room area. There was a breakfast bar that separated the kitchen and living room, but then once you were in the kitchen it expanded back a bit and there was a quaint eat in area and beyond that a door that led outside to a small patio.

She reached for his hand once they were seated and he was caught a little off guard, his eyes darted over to her. Then she closed her eyes said the blessing, then released his hand. They started eating and he was surprised at how much this dinner felt like real comfort food. Not that he ever really remembered it as that...but this whole meal had that feel to it, and unexpectedly he liked that feeling. It was tasty, robust and yet light, he even had seconds, and the toasty bread did not appear to be a problem. There was only one small piece left in the basket once they had finished eating; each being too polite to eat the last piece.

Their conversation was light covering a wide variety of topics. Mainly he asked about her life and interests, it allowed him to gain a glimpse into her world and the way her mind worked. Which after talking with her for a bit he was not sure he would ever be able to completely figure her out. Maggie was so different than the other women he had spent time with, she was an enigma, and he kind of liked it that way. After finishing his meal he stood up, then went over to the sink to rinse his plate before placing it in the dish strainer.

"Thanks, just leave your plate there and I'll finish up later. Did you get enough to eat?"

"Yes. Yes I did, it was delicious. Feel free to make me spaghetti anytime."

"I'll make a note of that." She said smiling.

He dried his hands on the dish towel that hung on the oven door. Maggie moved around him to rinse her own plate and laid it next to his. She gestured for them to move back towards the den, turning the music down a bit so that they could talk. Sebastian sat on the couch and leaned back crossing his legs. She sat down at the other end of the couch, turning sideways to face him pulling one of the throw pillows into her lap.

"Again thank you for dinner. I really enjoyed it. And thank you for agreeing to meet with me."

"Sure. So what do you have on your mind Mr. Petersen?" She inquired in a mock seriousness, admiring his strong facial features.

"I am aware that Ava's injuries will take several weeks to heal and a couple more for her to get back up to her normal speed. She has a business to run and I know you are instrumental in assisting her with her business. I also know you are getting into your busy season so I would like to offer Candace's services at La Noel. She is a wiz at retail, and I think she could be a huge help to you during the holidays. She is gifted in the ways of wrapping paper and all things ribbon." He said grinning. Maggie was chewing on her thumb nail as she listened to him state his case.

"Wow. I wasn't expecting that. I mean I am going to need help that is for sure, but I'm not sure what I could pay her, I would have to discuss that with Ava." She said contemplating his offer.

"I'm sorry if I was not clear. We would pay Candy to work for you. She is already on Miles's payroll, so we would just loan her out to you until Ava is back on her feet."

"Oh, I see. Well maybe we could try it for a couple of days to see if we click or not, and see if she likes the store? Would that be ok?" She asked tentatively.

"Yes of course, that is a reasonable request. My second order of business is that unbeknownst to Miles and Ava, they both had requested that the Plumbing store space be shared between them. Mr. Anderson, the landlord, has agreed to that but neither of them know of that decision yet. So, my father and I would like to start construction based off the layout that was submitted, and hopefully have it finished before Christmas. We would also like your input on Ava's half of the space in regards to the storage that is needed so that it can be maximized. I'd like to surprise them with this, if we can pull it off. We are going to tell them the space was leased to an unknown third party, and that they are doing the renovations to hopefully throw them or at least Miles off track. They both need a bright spot to focus on and I think this might do the trick. So are you in?" He asked studying her reaction with a serious expression on his face.

She shifted slightly, picked at one of the threads on the pillow then bit at her lower lip. Not quite the reaction he was expecting.

Shifting slightly uncrossing his legs and rubbing his hands on his pants with them ending up folded in his lap.

"Are you doing all of this to make up for what you did wrong?" She asked softly still looking at the thread on the pillow and not into his eyes. He paused before answering.

"Perhaps." He replied, her question catching him off guard. "However after much reflection, I do believe it is the right thing to do for my brother and for Ava. I do not expect that this will absolve me from the wrongs I have done. I am not sure what will at this point." He said without emotion.

"I think asking for forgiveness is the first step. From the Lord first, then from the injured party. God is faithful to forgive and He never brings it back up again. It is removed as far from the East is from the West. I pray God will give you peace Sebastian." She said lifting her soulful brown eyes to meet his, and they both just looked at each other for a minute or so before she spoke again.

"Yes! I am on board with this plan. I too think it is the best for both parties involved, and I am pleased that your family thinks so as well. Thank you for including me, I know you didn't have to."

"Well, thank you for dinner. I will let you know when we are ready to get started." His tone was cordial but distant. He stood and reached for his jacket then headed for the door. Things between them turned chilly.

"Sebastian?" She said looking up at him, her enormous brown eyes reflecting confusion. She also stood and tossed her pillow back on the couch. He turned and looked back at her, his expression was one of all business. That is what he reverted to when he was uncomfortable or unsure of his situation. It's where he was comfortable and could maintain control.

He gave her a nod and then walked out the door. She walked over to the doorway and watched him walk all the way out to the car and get in. He never looked back or up in her direction once he got in the vehicle. She closed the door wondering what had happened as she headed into the kitchen to clean up from dinner.

Sebastian slammed his fist against the steering wheel as he pulled away from her apartment complex. *I know what I did to Ava was cruel, but am I going to have to apologize for it for the rest of my life? Maybe I deserved that comment from her? I don't know...* He thought he and Maggie were getting along well, and it hurt more than he cared to admit that she had questioned his motives. *I'll just keep things light and business like, Miles will be back in the saddle soon enough. Then I can get back to my life in the city.* He rationalized. Sebastian rubbed his hand over his chest, it felt tight and restricted. He breathed in deeply and exhaled slowly, repeating this pattern several times but it didn't seem to help.

Miles nodded off then his head dropped downward, which woke him back up. He lifted his head up slowly and then looked at his watch. Three a.m. He tried to shift to get comfortable again, but his foot had fallen asleep and it felt like a thousand needles were stabbing him. He sat up stretching his arms and hit the IV stand almost knocking it over. Ava reached out for his hand, which got his attention. Quickly reaching back for her letting her know that he was still there.

"You ok?" She whispered her eyes still closed.

"Yeah I'm sorry sweetie, I didn't mean to wake you." He stood and leaned over her and lightly touched her face.

"Are you ok, do I need to get the nurse?" He continued.

"Maybe, I'm having pain in my side, on the left over here." she replied breathlessly as her hand moved to where the pain was coming from.

Miles bolted out of the room and found Nurse Jenny down the hallway coming out of another patient's room. She followed him back to Ava's room he waited outside so that she could examine Ava. After a few minutes she emerged with a serious look on her face and called the attending physician. Ava had developed a fever and the left side of her abdomen had become distended. The threat of infection had always been a concern and now they needed to figure out what was going on. The doctor ordered blood work-Stat. So Nurse Jenny came back in and drew several vials of blood and had an orderly walk it down to the lab as a rush order. She also started an IV with antibiotics and gave her Advil for the fever.

Nurse Jenny then came over to Miles and checked him. He was running a slight temperature of 99.9, which was minimal compared to Ava's temperature 102.2. Still she felt compelled to treat him as well.

"Miles, I'm not sure if you have picked up something like a virus or not, but I'm going to need you to stay out of her room for a while until we determine what is going on with her. You are also running a slight temperature and I am not sure how we need to treat that, but I'd like for you to go down to the E.R. and be seen."

"Do you think I made her sick?" He asked horrified.

"No honey I don't think so, I believe hers is related to her accident, but I want to try and rule things out. The doctor wants her quarantined so no one can go in now without gloves, and full hospital garb." She explained sympathetically. Nurse Jenny and Tammy both had really grown fond of Miles and admired his devotion to Ava, she knew it would devastate him to think he had contributed to her discomfort.

"Ok, tell me what you want me to do."

"I'm calling down now to see if they can take you in and check you over. I know you are exhausted and your body is on overload. It could be as simple as that, but we need to make sure."

She proceeded to call down to the emergency room and they had two beds open so they could send him on down. They would assess him and let her know the results. Miles walked on down to admitting and they processed him quickly and got him back to a room. The nurse who took his vitals and weighed him in was a woman who went to his church, he did not know her personally but they would nod or say hello in passing.

"Miles Petersen. Boy we have all been praying for you and that sweet Ava at church." She stated as she put the blood pressure cuff on his arm.

"Thank you ma'am. It's been quite an ordeal, but the Lord saved her." He said giving her a slight smile.

"Yes! Yes he did. How are you holding up?" She asked as she wrote down the numbers that flashed up. Next she pulled out the thermometer.

"I'm fine."

She put the thermometer in and it read 102.1. "Hmmm I thought up stairs said that your temp was only 99.9, if that's the case, it has shot up in the last thirty minutes and that's not good. Why don't you lay back? The doctor will be in shortly."

Miles did not bother to protest, he was exhausted, and his head throbbed. When the doctor walked in, he did not even attempt to sit back up. The doctor came over took his wrist and checked his pulse, which was elevated. He asked Miles a few questions, did a brief exam then walked back out. The nurse came back in to swab his throat and nose then drew one vial of blood.

After twenty minutes the doctor reemerged announcing Miles had the flu and needed bed rest and medication. The nurse came back in to hand him the prescription and instructions for handling the flu. She informed him they had already called upstairs to let I.C.U. know since Nurse Jenny had referred him downstairs, and Jenny had called his father, who was on his way.

"What about Ava? Does she have the flu also?" He asked alarmed.

"I don't know Miles, but I will have them notify you once they do know what is going on. Go home and get some rest."

He sat there on the edge of the bed feeling like he had been hit by a truck. Not only that, he didn't get to tell Ava goodbye and was feeling lost. When he called up to I.C.U., Nurse Tammy answered.

"I.C.U. Tammy McCall speaking"

"Hi it's Miles..."

"Oh Miles, we are so sorry you are sick honey. We have your things and will hold onto them for you. They won't let you back up here on this floor until you are clear, you know that don't you?" She had cut him off.

"I guess that makes sense. I didn't get to tell Ava goodbye, is she ok?"

"Her fever has come down some, and she appears to be resting now. We will let her know where you are, and don't you worry. We will take good care of her. You just focus on getting better so you can come back up and see us."

"Thank you for everything."

"Certainly! Feel better soon, ok? Bye honey."

New Beginnings

The nurse came back in to announce that his father had arrived and was waiting for him. He slowly got off the table and exited the room with his paperwork. His dad was fully dressed and shaved and it was only five thirty a.m. Amazing. He felt a little embarrassed that his father had to come pick him up, but then he remembered that Sebastian had his Rover due to the poor weather conditions while his BMW was safe and snug in the family garage. Miles's mother also drove a new Land Rover Range Rover, and that is what his father had driven to the hospital.

"I'm so sorry you feel so poorly son. Let's get you home. I'm going to drop you off and then have someone pick up your prescriptions for you." He said taking the paperwork from Miles and leading him out to the car.

"Thanks dad for coming, I had no idea they had called anyone."

"Of course. I'm taking you to the main house, the Weston's have gone back home so the guest room is available. That way your mother doesn't have to walk up to the cottage to check on you. We will make sure you have your things."

"Its fine, I'm fine. Thank you." He laid his head against the cold window pane. One minute he was freezing and then the next he was hot. The ride home seemed quick and the roads appeared to be better this morning than they were when Sebastian had dropped him off last night. His father pulled into the garage then came around to get Miles's door. He was so pale and honestly his father was afraid he was going to pass out before he could get him inside the house. Between the sheer exhaustion of the last forty eight or so hours and the fever and flu symptoms, Miles's body was on overload. No wonder he slept so much yesterday.

Thomas managed to get Miles to the guest room then helped him get undressed and settled. He laid back on the pillow, his brow was completely covered in sweat, yet he was shivering. He left him lying there and went to find his wife. She was in the kitchen making some hot tea with honey, and Candace was scurrying around trying to make her lunch and get ready for work.

"Sweetheart, I have Miles set up in the guest room. We may need more blankets in there, check on him and I will get the blankets down for you. He is really sick and weak, please don't try to get him up without help. You have had your flu shot haven't you?"

"Yes, along with my pneumonia shot. I will be fine, don't you worry about me. I am going to take him some tea and honey so that he can take some Advil. Or did they give him some at the hospital?"

"I am not sure they did not say nor did he mention it. I would take some in there just in case." He walked over and handed her the paperwork from the hospital then kissed her lightly on the lips.

He walked down the hall and took down a couple of blankets then put them in the chair in the guestroom. Miles was just lying there with his eyes closed with a pained expression on his face. Thomas noted that Miles was always the 'suffer in silence' kind of child. He remembered when Miles was eight years old and fell getting off his horse, his foot had gotten tangled in the stirrup and he dropped hard on the ground. He laid there holding his arm but never cried. It was only when they set it at the hospital that he cried out slightly and a single tear slid down his cheek. Thomas walked back into the kitchen and announced the blankets were in with Miles.

"Are you staying at the office all day today?"

"I am not sure, I have a few meetings that I am taking for Sebastian so he can be here at the Café. I should be home by six or so, but I will call you."

"I love you, be safe." She said kissing him again.

"I love you. Let me know how Miles is doing this afternoon and if I need to bring anything home for him"

"I will."

"Bye Uncle Thomas, have a great day!" Candace chimed in as he walked out the door. He smiled and waved back at her. Having a high energy girl in the house full time now was certainly a change for everyone. She was exuberant and talked non-stop which was something new for everyone in the Petersen household. She was trying so hard to be helpful and be a good house guest. It was evident she was taking Miles's words to heart and was attempting to become a productive member of society. It had only been a few days, but she was giving it her best shot.

Chapter 12

Dude

Ava's parents arrived at the hospital right at shift change so the nurses were trying to get them up to speed on Ava's condition as well as Miles's before they left for the day. Ava seemed to be responding to the antibiotics so that was a good sign. They still had to suit up before going in to see her, washing their hands and putting on gloves. She seemed to be resting and her parents were grateful to the staff who were so attentive and proactive with her. They were concerned that Miles had given Ava something and were glad that he had gone home for now. Maggie came by for a quick visit before opening the store and was alarmed that Miles was not there. She had hoped to speak to him about Sebastian's reaction last night.

Mrs. Turner came out into the hallway to speak with Maggie still wearing the mask, coveralls and gloves.

"What's going on with all the gear?" Maggie said incredulously. "What's wrong? What happened last night?"

"Well Ava started having pain with fever in the middle of the night, so they sent Miles down to the E.R. to have him checked out and he has the flu! They sent him home so that he doesn't infect Ava anymore. I was worried about him being up here all the time anyway. Doesn't he have a job? How does he stay out of work like that?" She remarked coldly which did not sit well with Maggie, who came flying to his defense.

"Anita I don't think I like your tone regarding Miles. I realize you don't know him like the rest of us do, and I think you are a little jealous of his time with Ava. He loves her and is completely devoted to her, he would never do anything to cause her harm. He is a great guy, and a *very* hard worker. He owns the Café where he works and his brother Sebastian is working in his place so he can be here with Ava."

"He owns it? I thought he was just a manager there. Maggie I'm not trying to say I don't like him, I just don't want him up here if he is sick. I have to think about Ava." She stated indignantly.

"That is what I am saying, he would never do anything to hurt her, and he did go home as soon as he realized he was ill. The doctors said that she could run a fever due to injuries from the accident and I'm sure that is what's wrong. I've got to go open the store, I'll call later and check in on her." She turned and left the I.C.U. frustrated with Anita's attitude. Anita stood there stunned. *Who is this Miles that has everyone so enamored and charmed? First Ava, now Maggie.*

Rob Turner walked out into the hall and saw his wife standing there staring in the direction of the elevator.

"What's going on out here?" He asked looking back at the nurses who heard the whole outburst, and now where acting busy. "Anita?"

"Well I guess I upset Maggie when I said I was glad Miles went home since he was sick."

"Honey I know you resent all the time he spends up here with her. I know you feel like it's your job to attend to her not his, but try and think about how he feels. It is obvious that he is crazy about her, and would do anything he could for her. He's in love. Apparently so is she, did you not see how her face lit up when he walked into the room? She loves us and she always will, we are her parents, but she is *in* love with him. I walk around this hospital and it doesn't matter where I go, when I ask about Miles Petersen, there is never an ill word about him. Everyone loves him, and thinks he is the real deal. You need to give him a chance."

She folded her arms not liking the idea that her own husband was now siding with a very emotional Maggie. "I never said I didn't like him." She huffed.

He walked over then put his arm around her shoulder and suggested they go down to the cafeteria to get some coffee. She nodded and they walked over to the elevators. The nurses looked up at each other will a telling glance and grinned. Thankfully Mr. Turner had Miles's back.

Maggie arrived at the store around eight a.m. and since they don't open until nine, she went into the Café to get her coffee. Entering she made haste walking over to the counter to place her order. Tim was behind the bar today, since Natasha had a dentist appointment and would be in later. Candace was scurrying around wiping down tables and setting flowers in small vases on the tables.

"Good morning Tim. Surprise me today. I don't want the same thing. I'm a little worked up and want something different." She said in an animated fashion waving her hands wildly about.

"Then different it is, one Tim special coming up." He said grinning.

Sebastian thought he had heard her voice so he hesitated in the office. His pride was still smarting from their dinner last night. He stood in the doorway, then slowly walked out. He noticed today's ensemble under her long tan coat was navy leggings, black ankle boots, a long navy, yellow and white tunic with a small print on it. Her hair was loose and curly with a clip on the side to keep her bangs under control. Smiling he acknowledge that she definitely had a flare and style all her own. As he rounded the corner she caught a glimpse of him, "Dude? There you are, I was wondering if you were here today. I hope you have had your flu shot." She rattled off in his direction. *Dude? Did she really just call me dude?*

"A flu shot? What are you talking about?" he asked thoroughly confused walking in her general direction.

"Your baby brother is home languishing with a high fever and the flu. They kicked him out of the I.C.U. ward and called your dad to come get him this morning. It's completely pitiful." She said reaching for her special coffee which smelled heavenly.

"Wow Tim, you may just have replaced Tasha as my favorite barista." She tasted and said with a wink. Tim grinned at her and saluted. He had a secret crush on Maggie and longed to ask her out but never had summoned the courage to do so. He for now remained content to see her occasionally and day dream.

Stepping around the counter then walking over towards a table Sebastian motioned for her to follow. She came along behind him and sat down. He felt slightly awkward like he wanted to reach across to touch her hand, but he refrained then sat down himself and waved Candace over.

"Hi Maggie. Sebastian said that I might work over at your store for a day or two. I think that would be great, just let me know when and I'll be there. I already know how to run the register, they've already showed me that here." She offered.

"Oh, Ok. Well that will be a good start, but our register is really different than the one here at the Café. They use different software, but the premise is the same, so as long as you can count out change and run a credit card machine, we should be good to go. Girl, no worries." She reassured. She could see Candy's eyes get big when she stated the registers were different. She looked over at Sebastian and he gave her a sympathetic look.

"Oh I didn't know there were different kinds, but I'm sure I can learn it."

"Of course you can, it's not a big deal. Really I don't want you to sweat it. Right Sebastian?" Maggie said reaching over and grabbing his arm. He looked at her hand on his arm and merely nodded in agreement.

"I can come tomorrow morning if that is ok with you. Sebastian is that ok?"

"If that suits Maggie's schedule, I'll let you two work that out." He started to rise when Maggie quipped, her hand still on his arm, "Dude where are you going? I am not finished with you yet." To which he immediately sat back down and Candace commented she would see her at nine sharp tomorrow then went back to work.

"I'm sorry, I did not realize you had unfinished business with me." He stated in a mock formality.

"Listen, I am sorry if I offended you last night. I have a tendency to say what I think immediately when I think it, and my filter doesn't kick in until after…when it's too late." She said quietly. "I feel like we have gained some common ground lately and I don't want to mess it up with my big mouth. Please accept my apology."

"Maggie, we are fine." He said with a courteous fake smile.

"Liar! I can see it in your eyes. I did hurt your feelings! Sebastian, you have to tell me." She said raising her voice in a loud whisper. Sebastian, who was completely uncomfortable with airing his emotional dirty laundry at all, let alone in the middle of a public Café, shifted in his seat and then their eyes met. For a moment he was lost in her big immense round chocolate eyes and paused. He took a deep breath, and when he exhaled she grabbed his hands holding them in hers.

"Ok. Yes....Maggie I was hurt last night. I am so very sorry for things I have said in the past, and I wish I could take it all back. Yet I just feel sometimes like I will have to make apologies for it for the rest of my life. I'm really trying hard and I just feel discouraged." He said quite contrite.

"Thank you for telling me the truth, which is all I want from you. The truth...always. Got it?" She said smiling patting his hands.

"Yes ma'am. I think I understand." Grinning himself.

"Don't you feel *so* much better having shared that with me?" She stated a little too exuberantly.

"Actually, no. Now I feel odd and self-conscious." He stated calmly. She burst out laughing then reached over hugged him. "Honesty. I love it!" She said still laughing. "I have to go to work now, and you better get busy around here before you get fired." She got up and shouted her goodbyes to Tim and Candace then sauntered back to the La Noel.

Sebastian quietly walked back to the office still not entirely sure what had happened out there, but he was fully aware he had bared his soul to a woman he hardly knew in a public place. He hoped this would not become a habit.

Mary Beth checked on Miles and was worried that his fever was not dropping below one hundred and was spiking. He was tossing and turning in his sleep and she could see he was not resting well at all. Her poor baby all six three of him was dripping in sweat, his hair matted to his forehead. The medicine thus far was not making a difference, and that had her worried. She kept placing cool cloths on his head and had placed a call into his regular physician. She called Thomas to fill him in on her afternoon and he also heard the worry in her voice. He promised to finish this last call and head home immediately. She walked back into the kitchen to make more tea then heard the front gate buzzing.

"Yes may I help you?" Mary Beth spoke through the speaker.

"Hello, yes I am a friend of Miles's and I wanted to check on him please. I have some things of his from the hospital."

"I will buzz you through and drive past the barn to the circle drive then come to the front entrance."

"Ok! Thank you." Maggie heard the buzz and then the gate swung open. She slowly drove her VW beetle through to the circle drive way. *This place is amazing! I can't believe they grew up here.*

She walked up to the front porch then rang the doorbell. After a moment, the door open and there stood Mary Beth. Tall and so elegant looking, Maggie could see where the boys got their lovely eyes from.

"Hello, so you are a friend of Miles's?"

"Yes ma'am. My name is Maggie Willis. I work at La Noel with Ava, she is my best friend."

"Oh dear, please come inside," she said stepping forward and hugging Maggie then taking Miles's duffle bag from her hand.

They sat in the kitchen talking enjoying a cup of tea for about thirty minutes or so before Thomas came home. Mary Beth made quick introductions and then he walked back to his office. Maggie stated she needed to get going and said that she would be praying for Miles. Mary Beth walked her out and told her she was welcome to visit any time. Maggie drove out the long drive way passing Sebastian on her way out, piquing his interest even more.

Maggie drove home then ate the remaining spaghetti for supper. She had planned to check in on Ava, but really wasn't ready to see Anita Turner again today. She loved her like a second mom, but she was being selfish and narrow minded. That really got under Maggie's skin, because Anita was better than that. When she called to check in, Rob answered. He informed her that Ava was responding to the medication and her fever was down. Maggie filled him in on Miles's condition and he was very concerned and said to give him their best. She stated that she was tired tonight, but would see them tomorrow. She hung up and then worked on her bible study lesson for Wednesday's class with her teen girls.

Sebastian and Candy arrived at home and while she went to her room to change, he went to check in on Miles. He tapped lightly on the door before entering the room. Seeing Miles laying there, with chapped lips, damp hair, and sheets that were completely soaked worried Sebastian. Miles looked so pale, so Sebastian slowly walked over to touch his brother's forehead which was still very hot with fever. He knelt down by Miles's bed and attempted to lift him up but Miles did not respond, so Sebastian took off to find his mother.

"Mother!" Sebastian called out.

She came immediately seeing the alarmed look on his face. His father followed behind her and they all met in the hallway.

"What's wrong?" She asked startled.

"I think we need to take Miles back to the hospital. He looks completely dehydrated which will only make his condition worse. I think we should call the ambulance."

"I've tried all day to get his fever down and to get him to drink...."

"Sweetheart it's not your fault, Miles is just very sick. Go call them, Sebastian and I will go back in with Miles." Thomas kissed her lightly on the cheek and smiled reassuringly.

The ambulance arrived within fifteen minutes and EMT's tried to start an IV but his veins kept collapsing due to the lack of fluid. They decided they would wait until they reached the emergency room to attempt again. The family followed behind in Mary Beth's car. Sebastian texted Maggie, *Taking Miles to hospital he is suffering from dehydration. Will update you when I can. ~ Sebastian*. She replied almost immediately, *I'm on my way. – Mags*

The family had to wait in the lobby while they admitted Miles into the E.R. Maggie arrived about fifteen minutes later. She stayed with the Petersen's until they placed Miles in a room and got the I.V. started. Then she went upstairs to check on Ava. She was looking better and was sitting up sipping on some broth. She was elated to see her friend, and wanted her to stay in chat. Maggie hugged her then told her that Miles was downstairs in the ER suffering from dehydration and the flu. Ava's face fell and she looked as though she was going to cry. "It's ok, they have started an I.V. and once they get some fluids in him, he will start responding. I just wanted you to know why he wasn't here. You know he loves you, right?"

"I feel horrible that he is so sick. I wish I could go to him"

"I know, but he's going to be ok. You have to get well yourself and get stronger. His friend Candy is going to help me in the store tomorrow and we will see how it goes. If she does well, then I may have her help out until you have recovered."

"Can we afford to pay her Maggie?" Concern shrouded her eyes. Maggie explained that the Petersen's were taking care of all that and not to worry. Ava seemed somewhat relieved, then demanded that Maggie go back downstairs and check on Miles. Then Ava blew her a kiss as she headed back downstairs. Rob stopped her on the way and wanted to go down to check on Miles too. Together they went back into the E.R., and Maggie introduced him to the Petersen's. The men shook hands then talked for a bit.

Ava walked in to Miles's room seeing Sebastian standing there just staring at a very sick Miles. She came alongside him and slid her hand into his. He looked down then squeezed her hand. She noticed that the look on his face was similar to what she witnessed the night of Ava's accident and it broke her heart. They just stood there holding hands neither of them speaking. Maggie closed her eyes then began praying out loud, asking for God to heal Miles and restore him back to his family and to heal Ava.

Sebastian just stood there holding her hand tightly as tears welled up in his eyes. He just wanted his brother well, and their lives back to normal. He was so moved by Maggie's gesture and once again stood there in awe of her. Mary Beth had been standing in the doorway witnessing the whole sweet scene. She was liking this Maggie more and more each time she saw her.

Mr. Turner and Thomas stood talking for a good twenty minutes or so before Anita made her way into the lobby looking for him. It had been a long day and she was ready to go home. He introduced her to the Petersen's and they chatted for another ten minutes or so before leaving to grab some dinner. Maggie came out so that Miles's parents could go in and spend some time with him. He was almost through one bag of fluids so the nurse came in to set another bag up per the attending physician. Mary Beth sat next to Miles and rubbed his hand. Nurse Jenny heard Miles had been admitted so she came down to check on him during one of her breaks. Introducing herself to the Petersen's she started sharing with them how great she thought their son was and how devoted he was to Ava.

Miles was about halfway through the second bag when he finally started looking better. Some color had returned and his fever was down a few points. The doctor said he would like to keep Miles overnight in an abundance of caution. He was awake so now it was his turn to receive the ice chips. Maggie came back with a cup full and fed them to him small spoonful by spoonful. Sebastian standing up against the wall, was suddenly wishing he had the flu. She stayed a few minutes then passed off the ice chip duty to his mother.

Maggie hugged Mary Beth then gave a small wave to Mr. Petersen.

"Dude, will you walk me to the door?" She said to Sebastian as she bumped him with her shoulder. *Dude? Really?*

"Certainly." He said with a nod.

They walked down the hall past admissions then out the front door. "I've got to ask, why are you calling me Dude?" Maggie grinned, then explained it was her way of making him less intimidating and loosening him up. Since it was such an unnatural association for him that is why she chose it. He shook his head flashing her a Petersen smile showing off his dimples, another thing he and Miles had in common.

"Good night, be careful going home." He said lifting and kissing her hand.

"I'll check on everyone tomorrow. Oh, and I'll let you know how Candace does at the store. Thanks again." Reluctantly she took her hand back then walked over to her vehicle. He stood outside until she pulled away.

Chapter 13

The Invite

The next few days had Miles returning home to recuperate, and Ava getting stronger, eventually moving into a regular room on the third floor. Ava spoke to Miles on the phone daily, also texting since he was stuck at home. Now that the weather had cleared a bit, visitors were starting to come by the hospital to see Ava. Her parents were touched by the outpouring of love shown for their daughter. Her father was scheduled to leave for Wisconsin in a couple of days and he was starting to miss Miles's company surrounded by all these women.

Mary Beth stopped by the hospital to check on Ava since Miles was still under quarantine. She happened to catch both of the Turner's there with Ava.

"Good afternoon!" Her smile was kind and inviting. Ava sat up waving her in, her mother Anita had been working a cross stitch loom and her father was watching the news. They both turned to greet their guest.

"Oh Mrs. Petersen, how is Miles today?" Ava eagerly asked.

"Sweetheart he is fine. Chomping at the bit to get back up here to see you, but he still is not eating enough. He has lost about ten pounds which has me concerned, but he is starting to get his strength back, so how are you? You look lovely today."

"Thank you! I was able to shower and wash my hair, so I feel like a new woman. Well actually I had help with my hair," she said glancing at her mother then back at her cast.

The Invite

After visiting for a few minutes, Mary Beth asked them to please join the Petersen family for Thanksgiving this year. Explaining they had more than enough space, and would love to have them over as a family. Anita agreed only if Mary Beth would let her bring a dish or two so the ladies stood hugging to seal the pact.

Mary Beth shared there would be approximately fifteen to twenty people including them, and they would be serving a ham as well as a turkey for the meats. She said that folks normally arrive between noon and one p.m., for appetizers and that they eat dinner around four p.m. They exchanged phone numbers and email addresses promising to stay in touch. Since everyone agreed it sounded perfect, Mary Beth stayed a few minutes longer, then excused herself to visit an elderly woman from her book club who was in for a heart by-pass surgery.

Miles was restless and weary from watching so much television, thankfully Zelda the faithful was by his side and she was a terrific conversationalist. Since he had shown up at the main house in his infirmed condition, she rarely left his side and he enjoyed her company. Candace was trying to be sweet by renting him movies and telling him about her escapades at the La Noel. He could just visualize her and Maggie holding down the fort with the hilarity that ensued on a daily basis. Maggie is a card by herself so that combined with the Lucille Ball like antics of Candy brought colorful images to his mind. Thankfully she and Maggie were getting along well, so the partnership for now seemed to be working out swimmingly. He received daily sometimes hourly texts from his crew at the Café and he missed them more than he ever could have imagined, but the void in his chest came from missing Ava.

He and Sebastian seemed to be getting along better, so for that he was grateful. Sometimes Sebastian would sit and watch part of a movie with him, or bring him something to drink. He wasn't smothering, but was reservedly concerned and Miles was enjoying the company. He couldn't remember the last time they had watched a movie together. Sebastian's life was so different now with all the international travel and business deals. Miles suspected he was up to at least four languages that he spoke fluently, plus a handful he spoke well enough to get by on the street. He admired his older brother's commitment and tenacity that it took to carry out that life style, and imagined that he must look like a slacker in comparison.

So far the secret had not gotten out about the store renovations, and Sebastian for one was stunned, especially with Candy. She had never been able to keep a secret, and from the time she was a toddler, both boys knew what they were getting for every birthday, Christmas or miscellaneous holiday due to her. They had become masters of the 'surprised' face and 'pretend' excitement.

Sebastian had not seen or spoken to Maggie for a few days, and was starting to miss their interactions. He sat back in the office making phone calls, setting up appointments in New York and Los Angelis for the week after Thanksgiving. He had enjoyed this brief respite from the grind of his grueling schedule, but it was time to get back to work. Several deals were pending and needed to be tidied up before the end of the year. There were moments he envied Miles and the relaxed way in which he went about his life, but great things were expected of Sebastian and he would not let his father down.

The construction on the building was coming along nicely, all of the demolition was complete and the clean-up was almost finished. They were starting on the plumbing which was going to be the largest part of the remodeling job tomorrow. The La Noel would be gaining two new toilets, double sinks, in the ladies room and a one stall men's bathroom with a sink. The Café would have a two and two on their side. The plumbing store had old hardwood floors that matched the originals that the Café had and were similar to what the gift store had installed so that worked to Sebastian's favor. Things at the Café were moving along like clockwork so overall the mood there was light and friendly. He and Natasha had even managed to exchange pleasantries in a couple conversations that were more than civil; especially after he gave all the senior barista's a raise. It never hurt to fan the winds of favor in your direction.

Miles meandered into the kitchen looking for a snack later that night. His appetite was starting to return so that was great news. Even though it was after nine o'clock, he decided to call in a pizza for delivery. The front gate buzzed about nine thirty and the delivery guy made his way to the circle driveway. Miles opened the door seconds before he could ring the bell, with Sebastian pulling up right behind

The Invite

him. "Perfect timing Miles... that smells divine." He said taking the pizza box out of his hand then heading into the den. Miles paid the driver, then watched to make sure he made it out of the driveway. He grabbed his drink and some napkins then followed the scent of the meaty supreme pizza to find that his brother was already half way through a second slice.

"Good grief, don't they feed you at the zoo?" He said laughing.

"I ate a turkey Panini and some pasta salad about noon, but I guess that didn't last." Sebastian said wiping his mouth with a napkin.

"I'm getting ready to watch *Midway* are you up for it?" Miles saw his brother hesitate, "Awe come on Sebastian, and you know it is one of the best war movies ever. A classic."

Sebastian nodded, kicked off his shoes then reached for another slice of pizza. As they were settling in on the couch with their drinks and pizza, Mary Beth wandered through remarking in her mom voice, "Good night boys, just be sure and clean up after yourselves." Her heart was happy to see them together and laughing in spite of what her den might look like in the morning.

"Yes ma'am" they replied in unison.

Maggie stopped by the hospital for a quick visit, and learned that both of Ava's parents were going back home for a few days. Her mom was going to be home for a day or two until she could get things together for a proper trip back to Mapleton. Ava's father had some business dealings and would not be returning until the Tuesday before Thanksgiving. She shared how well Candace was doing at the store, and that she was really good at organization. For once Candace was making sense of that storage area.

"Oh Mags, did Mr. Anderson ever get back with us on the space?" It was going to be hard for Maggie to look into those big blue eyes and lie to her best friend. She justified it by it only being a temporary lie, since as soon as the renovations were complete the cat would be out of the bag.

"Oh hey, yeah... I didn't want to upset you with all this accident stuff going on," she gestured with her hands. "Apparently there was someone else besides you and the Petersen's that were interested, so since you both had a store front on Main Street already, he decided to give the new guy a chance." She tried not to talk to fast and sound convincing. Lying was not her thing as she usually wore her feelings on her sleeve.

"Oh Ok. I guess that's fair. I'm disappointed, but hey there will be a new opportunity on Main, right?" Ava stated trying to conceal her worries.

"Well I've been talking to the brothers Petersen and they have a couple of great ideas for the store once you are feeling better. So don't worry about it baby girl! We've got your back." Maggie walked over and held her friend's hand giving her a reassuring smile.

Maggie could see Ava was getting tired and with the information about the store front trying to sink in, she thought she would head home. Ava promised to rest then mentioned that Miles might even get to stop by tomorrow since it's been a week, and he is no longer contagious. If the doctor clears him that is…..

Sebastian's phone started buzzing and when he looked down he realized it was Maggie. Trying to sound nonchalant "Hello this is Sebastian." Miles looked at him and asked if he wanted him to pause the movie, but Sebastian waved him off.

"Oh-my-gosh! Sebastian! I just had to lie to my best friend!" She spewed out and then tried to catch her breath.

"Ok, so what was said?" he replied calmly.

"Just that a third party had gotten the bid and that ya'll didn't get it either. I mean she seemed to take it ok, but wow, I have never had to lie to her before, but I think we are ok, I just wanted to let you know she knew something now." Maggie stated in a pant.

"Ok, that all sounds fine, I'm watching a movie with my brother right now."

"Oh, Ok. I gotcha. So talk to you tomorrow?" She inquired a little calmer now.

"Yes, that sounds fine, have a good night." He was grinning from ear to ear when he put his phone back in his pocket. *She is a trip! How refreshing to find a woman who frets about lying and scheming instead of living to tell a lie and get by with something. That's a switch.*

"Everything ok?" Miles asked.

"Oh yeah, sure. No worries. Hey are you still under quarantine from the hospital?"

"I go back to Dr. Evan's tomorrow for a follow up. I am fever free, feeling better but still my energy level is not back up. It's been a week now, so I certainly hope he clears me. I miss seeing Ava like crazy."

"I'm sure. I envy you Miles. You have found the perfect woman for you, just like mom is for dad. I just don't ever see that for myself." His words trailing off.

"Sebastian! Man don't say that. It's all timing. There is a perfect woman out there for you, I just know it. Don't give up yet, she will most likely show up when you aren't looking for her."

"I hope you are right brother, I hope you are right."

After his run the next morning, Sebastian dressed casually then made his way to the hospital to see Ava. It was time, she was getting stronger and Miles was feeling better. Now was the time to truly test his metal. Miles's appointment was at nine thirty, so he felt like he could get in and out before Miles arrived to see Ava. He tapped lightly on the door, and then poked his head through the crack. She was finishing her breakfast of grits, applesauce and apple juice.

"Good morning Ava, am I interrupting?" he said from behind the door.

"Oh no, please come in Sebastian." She said pleasantly. He was a little surprised by her tone, but thanked her and came into the room.

"How are you feeling? Your color looks good." He offered.

"I'm getting stronger each day, and my headaches are going away. I'll be happy when they let me go home."

"I'm sure. Ava I have some things I need to say to you and I'm not sure how to…"

"Sebastian," she interrupted. "How are *you* doing? Really? I want to know." She motioned for him to sit next to her.

"I'm not sure. What I said to you before in the Café was completely horrible, I was jealous and there is no excuse for what I did and how I made you feel. Then all the angst with Miles, it has been a roller coaster ride I would pay dearly to get off of. I feel like a leper.

I want so badly to make this up to you and to Miles, and I *will* find a way to make it up to you."

"So you are sorry for what you said to me and the trouble it caused?"

"Yes. More than I will ever be able to articulate, the guilt, shame and hurt is almost debilitating at times."

"Sebastian, I was hurt I won't lie, but I do not want this for you. I accept your apology, I just want you and Miles to have the relationship I know he longs to have with you. He really looks up to you."

"I feel like I'm being let off the hook too easily. By Miles, and now by you...." He said casting his eyes downward and folding his hands.

"Sebastian, Miles and I are not vengeful people. I believe you are sorry for what you did and that it won't happen again. We just want to get on with our lives and would like for you to be a part of them. If we are wishing ill for you or wanting revenge, what kind of relationship would that be? Certainly not one that Miles or I want to be a part of that's for sure. God forgave us of our sins when will were still wallowing in them Sebastian, so who are we not to forgive others who have wronged us?"

Sebastian stood and hugged Ava. She squeezed him really hard then patted his back, she could feel him relax a bit and that made her smile. "People love you Sebastian. Let them." She whispered.

"Thank you Ava. Truly for being so kind, and for loving my brother in spite of his relations." He said with a wink and smile. He stepped back a bit but was holding her hand.

"So are you trying to steal my girl now?" Miles said filling the door way.

Sebastian stood straight up and dropped Ava's hand so quickly it was almost comical. Ava put her hands on her hips and retorted, "Well look who finally showed up to the party?" Miles was completely focused on Ava, and she was having trouble holding a straight face then burst into a full smile. He walked over and playfully punched at Sebastian's stomach then kissed Ava lightly on the lips.

"So I guess the doctor cleared you?" Sebastian inquired.

"God you look amazing honey." He said to Ava. "Sebastian, I wasn't expecting you, and yes! I went in early and he worked me in."

The Invite

"Miles, I just woke up and look frightening. I'm so pleased Sebastian decided to stop by to see how I was doing. When I break out of this joint, maybe we could all go out to dinner? I would really like that." She smiled and wink at Sebastian. To which he nodded and grinned as his reply. The brothers shook hands, then Sebastian said he would talk to them both later.

Ava scooted over in the bed making room for Miles to sit with her. She was so petite at five one and hundred pounds soaking wet there was plenty of room for them both. He put his arm around her and nuzzled her neck. He had missed her so badly. They sat back talking for hours, until the nurse came to run some routine tests and brought her lunch. Miles excused himself and popped upstairs to I.C.U. to see if Nurse Tammy or Jenny were there. He caught Jenny and they spoke for a few moments. She was happy to see he was feeling better and said that she had been keeping tabs on Ava.

Miles stopped back by Ava's room and told her he was going home to rest but would come back this evening. He promised the doctor, otherwise Dr. Evan's would revoke his release. He leaned in tenderly kissing her, she stated said that she was due for a nap and would rest while he was away. It was hard to resist the temptation to show up at the Café and check in, but he was starting to get a little tired so he didn't want to risk anything that might keep him away from Ava.

He arrived at home and went straight back to his temporary room. Lying back on the bed once again his thoughts turned to Ava. *I'm going to ask her to marry me. Even though we really haven't technically dated, we have been together for nearly two years. I haven't dated anyone and she hasn't either, so I think I'm going to just throw it out there.* His mother heard him come in and waited for him in the kitchen but he never came. The door was open so she lightly tapped on it, seeing he was deep in thought about something.

"Are you hungry my son?"

"No not really. I know I probably should be, my pants are all but falling off me now. I just don't have a taste for anything."

"Well I have made a lovely tossed spinach salad with grilled chicken and there is plenty for you if you decide you want something that's light but has protein."

"Thanks mom. Maybe."

"What's on your mind Miles? I see those wheels turning."

"I want to ask Ava to marry me. I love her and with nearly losing her, I can't stand the thought of not seeing her every day. I compare everyone I see or meet to her and they all pale in comparison. She is one the best people I know, so loving, kind, and fun. It's her mom, she is the one."

"Well if you are serious come see me later, I have something for you. I have saved it for just this occasion."

"Ok, I'm gonna rest for a bit then I'll come find you."

She gently pulled the door to, then started back towards the kitchen when Zelda came trotting past her and head butted the door jumping into bed with Miles. *I hope Ava loves dogs,* she mused as she entered the kitchen. Mary Beth finished her lunch and then made a few phone calls. She was in charge of the music for this year's Christmas cantata at church and rehearsals were already underway, so they needed to discuss the reception in the fellowship hall afterward. Once she completed her calls she padded down to her bedroom and went into her walk in closet that also held their jewelry safe. In it were things she wore regularly and wanted to keep close, most of the family heirloom pieces were in the safety deposit box at the bank. All of it was insured.

She reached in and pulled out four boxes, all containing diamond rings. The first dark blue velvet box contain a pear shaped one and a half carat diamond in a simple white gold setting. The diamond itself was amazingly clear and unblemished and needed little fanfare to show off its detail. The next box contained a two carat solitaire in yellow gold. Either one would make a lovely engagement ring. The other two boxes held other diamond rings but after meeting Ava, neither seemed right for her personality or stature. She was petite with small hands, and a ring that was too big would seem showy and ostentatious which was not Ava at all.

She held those aside and would offer one of them to Miles if he wanted to go the family heirloom route with his token choice of promise. Mary Beth was beaming and could not wait for Miles to wake up so she could show him the rings. She was in full wedding day dream mode when he called for her from the living room.

The Invite

Looking at the clock she noticed it was four thirty and hoped he had rested well. He was starting to look better but still was not back to his old self. All of this turmoil had taken a toll on them, but some good was coming out of the near tragedy.

"Coming, go ahead and have a seat in the living room." She called back to him.

Miles sat on the sofa facing the fire place and gazed at the large reproduction oil painting of a lone woman walking down a lane along a brick half wall with a canopy of trees mostly void of their leaves giving her shelter overhead. There was something soothing about that picture, it always made him feel like he was home. Perhaps because it was one of this mother's favorites? He had looked at the picture at least a thousand times and never grew weary of it. Still an odd choice of art for a man his age, his father always said that Miles was an old soul.

Mary Beth sat next to her youngest and presented her rings giving him the history of each one and allowing him to examine them. "There is no pressure Miles for you to pick one of these, now of course I have dreamed of this day and have my own ideas, but truly this is for you. If you want it. If you would rather pick or design one of your own, I will be ok with that as well. Just be sure I get granddaughters so I can pass these down." She finished with a smile.

"Mom, I don't know what to say. These are so beautiful and I would be honored to have either one. I know Ava would love that it's a family piece." He kept going back to one in particular and eventually handed the other back to his mom.

"I feel this is the one. I can see it on her."

"Miles, sweetheart, I know she will love it. If nothing else because you picked it out."

They stood and embraced then Mary Beth walked back to her room with tears in her eyes. Her baby was getting married and she was elated. She looked forward to having another female around to help wrangle these Petersen men. She hoped that the Turner's would be as pleased with the match. Thanksgiving will let us know what the temperature will be, cold as ice or warm and toasty. She hoped for the latter.

Miles took one last look at the ring then took it up to the cottage and placed it in the night stand near his bed. He sat and prayed over the ring, asking the Lord to give him wisdom as to when and where to ask Ava, and her parents. He just wanted everything to be perfect for the one he loves. He changed shirts then went back to the hospital to see Ava for the evening.

Chapter 14

Jet Set

Maggie stopped by the Café in hopes of catching Sebastian. She thought he was going to call or swing by today but she had not seen hide nor hair of him. She swung the door open wide and waved at the evening crew. They saw her looking around and pointed back to the office. Maggie walked slowly back to the office area and thought she heard Sebastian speaking French to someone. *Is he speaking French? I feel like I just stepped off the plane and landed in Paris, and he sounds completely fluent. That is so cool!*

She stood in the doorway with her mouth open just watching him move and talk, it was like watching a ballet. He moved so fluid and his voice was deep and smooth his accent perfect. Eventually he turned and saw her in the doorway. He waved her in, but she shook her head and stayed put. She didn't want to interrupt him, mainly because it would have been rude, plus she enjoyed watching him work. He was fascinating. He finished his call and turned to her, "Êtes vous m'espionne?" He asked with his eyebrow arched.

"Ah……no?" she said shrugging her shoulders.

He broke out in a belly laugh standing there with his hand on his hips. "I asked if you were spying on me."

Maggie started laughing, "Oh, then yes! I was." Still giggling.

"I'm starving have you eaten?" He inquired as he put on his coat.

"No I haven't. What are you hungry for?"

"Well, I have to go back to my apartment for something father needs; care to tag along and keep me company? I will buy you food."

"Wow, you know how to woo a lady don't ya buddy?" She said with a twinkle in her eye.

"It's late, so we can eat first if you like. So what do you say?"

"I say…yes! Really was there ever a doubt? I know you can hear my stomach growling. So un-lady like." Her head cocked to one side with a loose curl escaping.

"Music to my ears mademoiselle," with that he took her arm and escorted her out to his car. It was a lovely night cold but clear. He turned the heat up, left the windows up and put the top down on the BMWm4 hard top convertible. She was very amused. Maggie sat back in her heated leather seat and thoroughly enjoyed the ride while Sebastian enjoyed showing off.

They ate at a quaint steak house that was known for their filet mignon, she had the six ounce and he had an eight ounce smothered in fresh sautéed mushrooms. The atmosphere was rustic and he secured them a table near the massive stone fire place. Very romantic. The background music was soft and light allowing for conversation. He was very animated tonight, which was a switch. She was more reserved and just soaking it all in, he was a true gentleman, opened doors, car doors, and stood when she got up to use the restroom.

Maggie tried not to swoon, this was Sebastian after all. He could have any woman he set his mind to. So she knew he was only being friendly and polite, but wow, to be his girl would be amazing. Just thinking of the places he travels to on business and vacations, not to mention he can afford to do almost anything he desires was overwhelming. This was not a world she was used to, she struggled to pay her rent and her modest car payment. Sebastian worked hard, but he played hard too, his lifestyle was far beyond what she dared at to dream of.

They finished dinner then he drove them to his apartment which was located downtown in a renovated manufacturing building. He was on the top floor, and the apartment was spotless just as she expected. The cool clean lines, leather and chrome furniture with modern art on the walls screamed bachelor pad. It was sexy and elegant, yet functional with a giant flat panel television, a top of the line sound system and a fantastic view of a botanical garden. Private parking in the covered garage and security cameras documented your every move. His kitchen was industrial and she longed to bake a cake in the magnificent oven which had probably never been used.

"Welcome to home sweet home." He said waving his hands around sweeping towards the den and kitchen open floor plan.

"It is exactly as I imagined your apartment would be, sleek and clean lines. Very modern." She said sitting on the couch.

"I'll be just a minute, I'm looking for a thumb drive and a file. I'll be right back, feel free to look around." He said heading in the direction of his bedroom.

Maggie stood looking at the pictures that sat on the faux mantle atop of the gas fireplace. There were lots of pictures of Sebastian with lots of beautiful people at clubs, or dancing, a yacht, eating dinner and fancy restaurants. It just reminded her of how different they really were, living in two totally different worlds. Miles lulled you into thinking they were normal everyday people, even the main Petersen house as elaborate as the estate was, it was elegant and comfortable. Mrs. Petersen made sure that everyone felt welcome there. Sebastian's life style was a world away from where she lived, so much so they might as well be from different planets. He certainly looked like he was having fun in the pictures, always a drink nearby and a beautiful woman even closer. He stood there watching her look at the pictures and wondered what was going through her mind.

"I found it. So we are off, or would you like a quick tour?" he said startling her as he walked up behind her.

"I'd love a tour, I must say this has my curiosity piqued." She shared.

"Well obviously this is the den and kitchen dining area. Over here is a full bath for guests, and over here past the dining area to the right is the guest room, laundry and to the left is my master bedroom and bath. Nothing along the size of the main family house." He stated almost embarrassed with the size of his apartment.

"Please Sebastian, this place is enormous. Lots of space, just not a lot of rooms chopping it up. Your bedroom is huge and then there is that nook over there I am assuming is your office? It's fantastic really." She marveled.

"Well I travel a lot right now, and this is practical. Eventually I would love to have a home, with land."

"I live in a closet compared to this place." She said turning a complete three hundred sixty degrees to look at everything in the room, soaking it all in.

"Please don't say that, I enjoyed being at your apartment, it felt very comfortable." He stated sincerely.

"I mean I'm happy there, you know? For now since there is just me myself and I living there, it works. Plus it is what I can afford since I want to go back to school to finish my nursing degree. That is my goal right now."

"I think that is fantastic. How much longer would you have to go?"

"I have my LPN, and I have another year into my RN but got side tracked with work and saving money, so I took two semesters off. I'm ready to get it finished up, so I have about another year to go maybe less if I go through the summer. Then I will have clinical rotations, after that.... Pass the exam and find a job." She smiled.

"Well I think you would make a great nurse. Good luck."

They walked back towards the front door and he armed the alarm as they exited the apartment. He walked with his hand at her back as though he was escorting her and she like the feel of his hand guiding her. It had gotten much colder outside so he left the top up for the ride home. They drove in silence for a few minutes and he had a dance music station playing softly on the satellite radio so they just listened to the music.

"Do you have a girlfriend Sebastian?" She asked out of nowhere.

"No. Not at the moment. Why do you ask?"

"Just curious, I cannot imagine you being alone for very long. I mean you are extremely handsome, wealthy, and smart so I'm sure women everywhere are just throwing themselves at you. Must be hard to fight them off. Good thing you know karate." Sebastian grinned in spite of himself. *She is serious too. I just know it.*

"Well, I do get a lot of that, I would be lying if I said otherwise. I'm sorry, I guess that sounds conceited, but I grow weary of that, beautiful women with nothing more on their minds that landing a rich husband so they can get off daddy's credit card and onto a paid ticket. I want someone with substance who loves me for me."

"No. It sounds honest. Well I hope you find a nice woman who will be kind to you and really appreciate how hard you work. You deserve that Sebastian."

"So what kind of woman do you see me with Maggie?" Now his curiosity was piqued.

"Someone tall and very fit, most likely blonde, as that would be a striking contrast to your darker coloring. She would be amazingly beautiful of course, but elegant not trashy looking. She would wear expensive clothes and shoes, and have amazing jewelry. She would be a corporate lawyer or something like that, she would be smart and sharp just like you. I don't see you with a flighty socialite or a wallflower." She said gazing back out the window watching traffic go by.

"Wow. I have met a lot of women who fit that bill, but it's never lasted for the long haul. I guess between our busy schedules or competitive lifestyles it's just never worked out. I find your take on me interesting though."

"Well honestly I really don't know you that well, so I could be very wrong about it all."

"As I get older I'm finding that I want something different, but I am not sure what. I guess I'll know her when I find her." He smiled cutting his eyes over to her then letting his eyes settle there as he studied her profile, she was really attractive in a natural beauty sort of way. She had a heart shaped face, big brown eyes, and sexy loose naturally curly hair that begged to have hands run through it. She needed very little makeup to make herself look radiant, and he loved the few freckles that dotted her nose and cheeks.

He pulled into a parking spot along side of her older Volkswagen then got out and opened her car door. "Thanks again for keeping me company. I hope I didn't keep you out too late."

"No! Thank you so much for asking! Dinner was wonderful, I enjoyed riding in your car and seeing your apartment. I really appreciate it, talk to you later?" She said rolling her window down then starting her car.

"I'm sure we will talk tomorrow. The space next door is really coming along nicely. Be careful driving and please text me when you've made it home safely."

"I will, thank you again." She rolled up the window then waved as she backed up.

Sebastian stood there and watched as she drove away. He drove back to his parents' home and Miles pulled in right behind him; they walked in together sharing what each other had done for the evening. Sebastian found his way into his father's office and they talked about the information on the thumb drive he had brought from his apartment. When they finished, Sebastian had clear plans for how he needed to proceed in London. *Made it home, thanks again for dinner it was all fabulous. ~Mags* Looking down at his phone and smiling he began quickly texting her back. *You are very welcome-SP*

Miles entered the kitchen and fixed himself a sandwich, his mother came padding in behind him to make a cup of hot tea. She asked about his evening with Ava, and he shared he was reading Jane Eyre to her. Ava was still getting headaches when she read or watched too much television. The doctor said it should subside over time. Over all she was feeling much better, so they were now anticipating her getting out of the hospital in a couple of days. Her mother was not due back for about four or five days, since they had some pipes burst at the house. She was having to stay home in Wisconsin to tend to that while Mr. Turner was traveling.

Miles invited Ava to stay at the estate or offered to sleep on the couch at her house until her mother could get there. He cleaned up his mess in the kitchen then headed to bed. Sebastian finished up with his father and he also turned in early. The more he and his father talked it was becoming apparent he may have to travel much sooner than expected. They would know by tomorrow.

Ava was restless and missing Miles tonight. She had spoken with her mom and told her the good news regarding her eminent release. They chatted for a while then discussed their Thanksgiving plans and what they would make to take over to the Petersen's.

Her mother was warming up to the idea of them and to Miles. He really had been nothing but polite, not to mention Ava had indicated how much she loved him. At twenty six years old Ava was a grown woman and could make these decisions regardless of what her mother thought. However, Ava did not want a forced relationship, she wanted everyone to love each other and get along. Her father was totally on board and looking forward to having a son in law, since Ava was an only child. He would joke and say he needed another man to balance out the females in the house. Soon he would have his wish and although Miles had not proposed yet, Ava felt he would one day in the near future.

Candace arrived early at the La Noel with a latte in hand for Maggie. Maggie was touched by her thoughtfulness and they sat chatting for a few minutes before opening the store. Candace had been a huge help to Maggie, catching on quickly to the flow of the business. She was grateful for her help and the company. Candy was really a sweet girl, just a little spoiled, but honestly was willing to do anything Maggie asked of her. Whether it was sweeping, wrapping gifts, stacking boxes, or dusting. She jumped in with a good attitude and the customers really seemed to like her. It was a win-win all around.

Sebastian called requesting to meet her in the space next door to discuss the shelving situation. She walked over and waited for him in the construction zone. He arrived looking a little flustered, which was unusual for him.

"Hey are you ok?" She asked.

"I think I'm losing it. I just got into a heated argument with the baker about her muffins for the Café. *MUFFINS* for crying out loud! I need to turn this back over to Miles, and I need to get back to my job."

"OK now......its *alllll* going to be O-Kay." She said slowly and sarcastically, fanning him with the folder she had in her hand.

After saying it out loud he realized how ridiculous he sounded and started laughing at himself. He was still grinning at Maggie as he led her over to the shelving and storage area for Ava's store. They were in the middle of going over the plans when he got a phone call. He excused himself, then walked to the back of the space near the restrooms that were now finished and operational.

Maggie was amazed at how quickly it was all coming together and how much room they were going to have, it was fantastic. Miles's side was almost complete except for the furniture which should be there any day. The painters finished his side yesterday. They were waiting on the last of the storage units to be built on Ava's side, then they would paint and finish trimming it out. Miles and Ava were going to be so surprised and elated with how it all worked out.

Sebastian returned a little more somber so they finished going over the last revision for the shelving. Looking down at his watch and then back at her, "I'm sorry but I've got to run if we are finished here."

"Oh ok. Sure. Is everything alright?"

"Yes, I have to fly to London tomorrow so I need to make some arrangements. I may end up in Brussels as well, but that's in the air right now."

"Of course, is there anything I can do to help you?" She offered.

"Actually, yes. Can you take this markup of the shelving plans to Ricardo so his crew can finish this job? It should only take him another day at most. That would save me a trip since he is in the opposite direction of where I need to go." He said relieved.

"Of course, go do what you need to do, I've got this. You have done an amazing job coordinating all this, Miles and Ava are going to be thrilled. Anything else?"

"No. You are a doll." Before either he or she realized it he leaned in and kissed the top of her head. They both looked sheepishly at each other, then he took off. She stopped by the store to make sure Candy was ok, and then drove to Ricardo's office to drop off the plans.

When Sebastian arrived back at the Café Miles was there surrounded by staff and customers alike pummeling him with questions, hugs and well wishes. He looked like a rock star standing there with his adoring fans. The sight of it made Sebastian smile. He avoided the love fest and headed straight to the office to pick up his briefcase. He didn't have much time to get his things together and get to the airport if he was going to make his flight. As he was leaving, he caught Miles's eye motioning like an airplane, mouthing "London" so Miles nodded waving him on.

He was so grateful for the time Sebastian put into the Café so he could be with Ava. His staff looked no worse for the wear, which of course was his main concern. He did however have a text from Edna May regarding Sebastian and her muffins. He was not quite sure what that was all about, but was sure he would find out soon enough. He remained at the Café for about an hour or so, then decided he would take Ava lunch. Now that she was stronger and closer to being released he was allowed to bring in some items and she craved pizza. He ordered them a pie and left to pick it up so he could be there during her lunch time.

On his way, Miles walked down to La Noel to check on Candy and Maggie. Candy was running the store when he walked in, then about two minutes later Maggie came in through the back door. Maggie was thrilled to see him and gave him a huge hug and kiss on the cheek. Standing off to the side, getting caught up they were talking non-stop. She gave him a few messages then handed him a couple of cards that people had left for Ava. Upon hearing of Ava's car accident people would stop by dropping off food, desserts, and cards for Ava. They did not want to intrude at the hospital but they wanted her to know she was missed. It was all very sweet, the cards and well wishes really brightened Ava's day.

Candy was stunned with the constant outpouring of affection for Ava, she had never been a part of a community that reacted this way when people were sick or injured. In her world they might send flowers or a text, but that was about the extent of it. Yet these people after several weeks were still bringing food and cards. One kind man and his son raked all the leaves out of Ava's yard then hauled any leaf or limb debris away for her at no charge, just so that she would not have to worry with it when she returned. That is why Maggie love living in Mapleton, for the people and the relationships.

Miles arrived at the hospital while Ava was getting out of the shower. He stood in the hall for a couple minutes waiting for her to get dressed and settled. The smell of the fresh pizza pie permeated the entire floor and the nurses were eyeing him, dying for a slice. Ava could smell it too, so she was trying to hurry by tying her hair up in a knot although it was still wet and she only had one arm. She called him into the room just in the nick of time as he was being approached by the hungry hospital staff. They both just giggled then she crawled into bed while he set the box on the covers and they had a little hospital bed picnic. It was one of the best meals she had eaten in a long time.

"Miles that was amazing. I have been craving pizza and this thin crust veggie is just what the doctor ordered." She said going for another slice.

"Dr. Miles knows what's best for his gal." He said beaming.

"The doctor was in earlier today and said I might be able to go home this afternoon or tomorrow morning! I would really like to go to my house if that is ok? I miss my space."

"Absolutely. That is not a problem. Why don't you let me have your key so I can go over with Maggie and get some things ready since I know you need groceries? I want to make sure your house is warm and ready for you."

"You will have to get a set of keys from Maggie, mine went down with the car....." she said her voice trailing off.

"Right, I'm sorry. Ava, what would you like to do about a car? Have you thought about what you would like to get to replace your SUV?"

"Yes and no. Part of me would like to have a new car, but then I worry about the expense. I want something reliable. You know?"

"Well if you have some ideas let me know, I can get you some brochures then we can test drive some. Do you think you want another SUV or would you rather have a car?"

"I feel like I need the space of an SUV or a truck since I have the store with all the boxes and displays. I like the idea of a car and the gas mileage you can get with a more efficient vehicle. I am really torn."

"You know you are welcome to use our farm truck or my Rover anytime you need to haul something. If that helps?"

"Thanks, I just need to see what's out there and in my price range. I am not sure what insurance is going to do about totaling my vehicle out. I guess that will help me decide."

"Well when you are ready let me know. I'll be happy to help you in any way I can." He reached over and rubbed her hand with his fingers.

"I love you Miles. I don't know what I would do without you."

"Let's hope you never have to find out. I love *you* Ava Turner."

Ava was full after two pieces of pizza but Miles proceeded to eat four pieces, his appetite appeared to have returned back to normal. They talked for a bit more, then he left for the grocery store and to get things ready for her homecoming, since that was going to be sooner than later. He kissed her lightly, then took the pizza box out and headed back towards the La Noel to get a key. He passed a car dealership on the way back into town and swung through to pick up a few brochures for Ava to peruse.

Miles stopped back by the La Noel to pick up Ava's house key from Maggie. Then he stopped by the hardware store to make a copy of the key, then to the grocery store to purchase the basics. Coffee, juice, milk, fruit, yogurt, cereal and some items to make a few crockpot stretch dinners so that she would not have to worry about cooking. He also swept the floors, then changed her bed sheets and started a load of laundry. He wanted everything to be perfect for when she returned home. Later that day he went back by the hospital to pick up all her flowers, cards and gifts to take them back to the house. He set them out on her dining room table, then he spread the flowers around in her bedroom, the den and kitchen area. The house smelled heavenly.

She was going to be released first thing in the morning so he was going to be ready for her. He scrubbed her bathroom down, wiped the kitchen counters off, and then ran the mop over the floors to freshen them up. He finally sat down about eight thirty pleased with what he had accomplished. After locking everything up he gave her a quick call before heading back to his house for the night. Miles planned to be there early so that when they discharged her, she would not have to wait on a ride.

Chapter 15

Home sweet home

Five thirty arrived early the next morning, so Miles lumbered out of bed, showered then dressed. He had gotten spoiled sleeping in late these last few weeks and needed to get back on schedule. He made a small pot of coffee then fixed himself a cup to go, since Ava had texted him and stated the doctor signed the discharge orders. After they processed her orders she would be ready to leave. She got into the shower trying not to get her hair wet, she managed to get dressed and was sitting in the chair waiting on Miles. Ava was ready to be home and have access to all of her things.

Miles pulled around front and then proceeded to her room with a wheelchair he found in the lobby. She was grinning from ear to ear when he appeared in her doorway. A nurse came in right behind him with instructions and medication for Ava. She helped Ava into the wheelchair, who kept thanking her and waving good bye. Miles all but ran to the car with her in tow. He helped her into the Rover then made sure she was belted in securely, like he was attending to a child. She indulged him, realizing he was trying so hard to take good care of her.

The ride home was smooth with Miles driving slowly, careful to dodge any bumps or potholes. Ava was content to drive slowly and take in all the scenery. She had missed Mapleton with all the sights and sounds of the small town she loved. They pulled into the driveway and she let out an audible exhale. *Home, I'm finally home!*

He was so sweet and had made her homecoming so special with the flowers everywhere. He even had vegetable soup cooking in the crockpot so the house smelled divine.

"Miles thank you so much for cleaning and making everything so perfect for me." Walking over to him, she gave him a tender lingering kiss.

"Ava, I am just so relieved you are feeling well enough to be home. If there is anything you want or need, let me know and I'll get it for you. I don't want you lifting anything—Dr.'s orders." He said with a grin.

She found the car brochures on the coffee table so she sat on her sofa and began looking at the different models. He busied himself in the kitchen getting the ingredients together to make cornbread muffins to go with the soup that was simmering in the crockpot. He felt so comfortable there with her and could easily imagine being married and their life together. He was biding his time until he would propose to her, he was old fashioned and wanted to ask her father for her hand. It was important to him to have her family's blessing.

"Miles..." she called out. "I think I like the look of this Toyota Highlander. It's an SUV but not a big one and I think would be a nice sized vehicle for me."

"I liked that one too, and the price is reasonable." He called back. She made a face at the price comment, not in her book was that a reasonable price, but she thought *I guess it's all things relative. To him that probably is a reasonable price. I mean his father drives a ninety thousand dollar Mercedes for heaven sakes.*

"Well maybe I can find a used one with low miles. That price is a little much for my budget."

"When you are feeling up to it, we can go test drive a few. Honey don't worry about the price, I can help you with that, I want you in something that you want and something that is safe."

"Miles, I do not expect or want you to feel like you have to help me with a car. I mean I appreciate it, but I don't want you to do that. It's too much."

"Ava, please let me. I have been saving my money for years. I have driven the same Rover since I was a teenager because I love that old hunk of metal. We don't have to decide anything now, I'm just saying if you find something you love and it's a good fit for you, I don't want price to be an issue. That's all. I love you so I want to help if I can." He walked into the den then sat down next her draping his arm around her shoulder. She leaned into him and laid her head on his chest.

"I know... I appreciate your offer. I really do."

"If you are hungry I can fix you something, I know it's probably a little early for lunch..."

"I'm ok, I think I'll wait for lunch, it smells fabulous, and here I am the one owing *you* a home cooked meal." She said with a soft laugh.

They chatted while looking through all the brochures, even looking at a few vehicle options online. Then they settled in with a blanket over them and took a nap on the couch. She loved that their bodies were all stretched out and interwoven together, it was comfortable and she was enjoying their time together. Ava knew all too soon it would end and they would both be back to their daily work schedules.

Maggie left the store in search of lunch for her and Candace. She had an odd craving for seafood so she went to the local fish camp restaurant and got them both a flounder fish plate with French fries. On her way back to the store she was stopped at a red light and texted Sebastian. *Eating fish and chips in honor of you being in London. Ciao. ~Mags.*

They both ate lunch quickly while the store business was slow. They had been steady all morning so this slowdown was a welcome break. About an hour later Maggie received a text from Sebastian. *LOL Funny. I needed that-SP.*

Ava woke with a start, her casted arm was throbbing and that woke Miles up. They both looked at each other sleepily then Miles got up and stretched. He headed into the kitchen to check on the crockpot. It was twelve thirty so he started mixing the ingredients for the corn muffins then stirred the soup. Lunch was delicious and they both enjoyed the homemade meal. Miles did a great job preparing the food, and Ava was very impressed.

The week passed quickly and after a few days Mrs. Turner had secured the house in Wisconsin then arrived in Mapleton. Miles was back at the cottage and back to work at the Café. The first few days were brutal getting back on the early schedule, but soon his body adapted. Arriving the day before Thanksgiving, Bob Turner found his gals in full preparation mode for the holiday festivities that would be occurring at the Petersen's. Based on what he found in the kitchen when he walked in, there was going to be one heck of a spread and he was gaining weight just looking at it.

"Honey, you do realize you have nothing to prove to them don't you? We were invited for supper. It's not a contest. You've got enough food for an entire football team."

"Humph. Men. What do they know?" She said to Ava, scoffing at her husband.

"We're not competing daddy, we just want to make sure we pull our load." Ava offered.

"Even though we are guests, Mary Beth and I made a pact that I would contribute to the meal and I intend to bring more than just a pie." Anita stated firmly.

"Yes dear." He said shaking his head grinning. He thought it best to stay out of the cooking frenzy going on in the kitchen so he headed into the den where it was safer.

The Petersen household was also a buzz with activity. Mary Beth and Melissa were in full preparation mode and had the house decorated beautifully with fall decorations and candles everywhere. She loved decorating for the holiday seasons and had a partner in crime with Melissa. The large rhombus shaped dining room table was set exquisitely. The table was custom made and boasted of four sides that seated five people on each angle. With the leaf in, it could seat four more in the midsection. The dishes were bone colored stoneware with the cornucopia motif tastefully painted around the edges. The salad plate that sat in the center was a plain burnt orange color stoneware within the same complimenting pattern and the bread plate was a buttery gold color. Each place setting had its own mini salt and pepper shakers in the shape of a male and female pilgrim.

The table was colorful and whimsical. Not stuffy or overly fancy, Mary Beth wanted her guests to feel comfortable and relaxed. They were expecting approximately sixteen people, so it would not be necessary to put the leaf in place at this time. They had the Hors d'oeuvres planned and ready to go, basic stuff that the Petersen boys have loved from a young age, like spinach dip, pigs in a blanket with special spicy mustard, and mini ham biscuits the size of a half dollar and a bowl of fresh fruits with a yogurt dipping sauce. Mary Beth always strived to make this holiday beautiful but something that the kids could enjoy with kid friendly foods as well as the fancier fare. Even now that the boys were grown men, some snack food requests never changed.

Thanksgiving Day arrived the weather was cool and blustery but the sun was shining. People started arriving around noon. The first to show up were Max and his wife Ellen who were in from Kentucky. They actually walked over from the barn apartment, since they had arrived late the night before. Miles had already been in and out of the kitchen all morning stealing snippets of things as they were baking. Some things never change. Sebastian called and stated he would be bringing an unexpected guest, and he did not sound happy, but of course Mary Beth stated there was plenty and she was welcome.

The next to arrive was Natasha, Miles had invited her since she had no family in the area. She brought a nice arrangement of yellow mums and handed it to Melissa when she arrived. Melissa showed her to the den where Miles and Max were hanging out watching television.

Next to show up were the Turners. It took several trips before they had all their food brought in from the car. There was a green bean casserole, two pies, sweet potato soufflé, a corn casserole and a coconut cake. Mary Beth was overwhelmed by her generous contribution to the feast. The two women hugged and Melissa helped set the items along the island in the kitchen. Then there were introductions to be made all around. Sebastian and a very lovely woman snuck in the garage entrance ending up in the den. Miles's eyebrow arched and he mouthed *Daria?* To which Sebastian, who was standing behind her, winced and nodded. Miles shook his head and couldn't help but laugh.

Daria was from France but had worked as a British Airline stewardess for the better part of ten years. She always seemed to find Sebastian when she had a North Carolina layover whether he wanted her to or not. She and Sebastian ran in the same social circles, and although Sebastian did spend time with her in the past, it was a very distant past and one he wanted to forget. He never knew when she would show up in the middle of the night to take liberties with his hospitality and invade his life. He was too much of a gentleman to turn her away in the wee hours of the morning when she would show up. She usually took over his bedroom and he would retire to the couch. This time she promised to get a pick up flight to New York, then Paris and would not be staying long at all. He was not keen on leaving her unattended in his apartment so he decided to bring her to dinner, praying she would get the call…and soon.

Daria was nearly six feet tall with most of that height being legs. She had long straight dirty blonde hair that fell midway down her back, small wide set blue eyes and an angular face. She was attractive in an under fed model kind of way. Candace made a bee line for her the minute she saw her from the kitchen. Hugging and squealing in the hallway they finally made their way into the living room, immediately talking gossip and fashion. Candace met Daria years ago in London when she was on vacation with her parents and the Petersen's.

Everyone was noshing on appetizers while Natasha along with the men had wandered off into the billiards room and were playing pool. The other women were in the kitchen mostly fussing over last minute supper details. Ava's phone rang and it was Maggie.

"Hey Mags what's up?" Ava asked.

"On my way into the city to see if the S&W Cafeteria is open for Thanksgiving."

"What? I thought you were going to your parent's house?"

"No, they bolted out of town at the last minute to help some friends with a soup kitchen and forgot to tell me. So I am solo this year."

"Oh Maggie that is awful, I can't stand the thought of you going there and eating all alone…."

Mary Beth overheard Ava's part of the conversation insisting she ask Maggie to come have Thanksgiving with them. She all but took the phone out of Ava's hands.

"Maggie, sweetheart, this is Mary Beth. Please come join us for Thanksgiving, we have enough food to feed the entire county and I am setting a place at the table for you right now. So we will see you in a few minutes, ok?"

"Oh ah, yes ma'am. Why thank you so much. That is so kind of you."

"Nonsense! We love you too, so get on over here." Mary Beth handed Ava back her phone with a triumphant smile.

"Maggie?"

"Girl I'm getting dressed and will be there in five. Oh wait. How are they dressed? Fancy? Or in like jeans?"

"A little of both. I have on a knit top, leggings and boots. Does that help?"

"Totally. See you soon."

Maggie tearing through her closet found the new burnt terracotta colored knit dress she had purchased on sale, her brown opaque stockings and her brown leather mid-calf boots. She tousled her hair and spritzed it. One last look in the mirror at her sheer makeup, she added a little colored lip gloss and was out the door. She arrived at the Petersen's approximately thirty minutes later.

Ava met her at the front door with a big hug. She ushered her into the kitchen where the women were still gathered arranging dishes. All except for Candace and Daria. They were still entrenched in the living room engrossed in their own conversation. Maggie was being introduced to the other guests when Sebastian walked in to get more ice and literally paled when he saw her standing there. He looked at her longingly and thought she looked fantastic; she absolutely lit up when she saw him walk in the room. All the women noticed the interaction between them.

"Hi Sebastian." She said throwing her hand up in a small wave.

"Hi Maggie. I, uh, just came for more ice." Then he immediately dove into the freezer to fill up the ice container, and slinked out of the room trying to go unnoticed.

"Wow. That was awkward." She stated quietly to no one in particular looking down at the floor after he walked out. Everyone else, especially Mary Beth noticed his reaction and quickly distracted a hurt Maggie with a chore.

Mary Beth rang the dinner bell which gave everyone a warning that dinner would be served in thirty minutes. It was a Thanksgiving tradition they started when the boys were little. She grew weary of the *"mom is it time to eat yet?"* mantra that was spoken every fifteen minutes by one or both boys until it was dinner time. The bell let them know that they could finish what they were doing, wash their hands and then it would be time to eat. It seem to work well with adults too.

The women set the feast out on the kitchen island and side boards so Mr. Petersen could say grace at the table. They would form a line serving themselves buffet style, then finally taking their seats at the dining room table. Maggie and Ava could not help themselves snapping pictures left and right of the table along with decorations throughout the house with their phones. Neither had seen a home decorated as lovely for Thanksgiving and could only imagine what it would look like at Christmas!

Finally it was time to eat so everyone started milling in around the table, Candy walked over and gave Maggie a hug then immediately introduced her to Sebastian's friend Daria. *Sebastian's friend Daria?? Now I understand why he was acting so weird in the kitchen.* They both uttered "Nice to meet you" and then selected a place at the table opposite one another. Sebastian took a seat on one side of Daria looking visibly uncomfortable and Candace sat on the other side. This had Maggie wishing they had a kids table in the kitchen somewhere that she could slink off to, that was until Natasha came to sit on her right and Ava on her left. Maggie smiled then let out a sigh of relief.

Dinner was fantastic with all the different food contributions and the multiple conversations going on at the table. It was relaxed with people visiting, laughing and telling stories about one another. Sebastian was quiet and low key pushing his food around on his plate not wanting to make eye contact with anyone. His date ate very little and spoke even less. She kept watching her phone which was a little disconcerting and seemed rude to Maggie.

After dinner, plates were gathered and the younger women started doing the dishes and cleaning so the older women could sit and relax. They devised an assembly line with the large volume of dishes and were finished in no time. The younger women chatted, making their task fun and enjoyable. Daria was noticeably absent, and soon it was made known that she and Sebastian had left without so much as a goodbye.

Miles managed to steal away with Mr. Turner under the guise of giving him a tour of the estate. While they were walking near the stables, Miles shared his ulterior motive which was to get permission to ask for Ava's hand.

"Mr. Turner, I know that it seems as though Ava and I have not been dating for a long time per se, so that would be a true statement. However, we have been together, our lives intertwined for the better part of two, almost three years now. We started off as friends, then good friends, and it grew. This may seem sudden but it's a relationship that has been evolving for a couple of years now. I love her so much, and I want to spend the rest of my life loving her, encouraging her and being the best husband I can be for her."

"Son, there is no doubt in my mind that you love my daughter and would be an excellent husband and provider. Miles, I have no objections at this time."

He extended his hand to shake Miles's hand, then Miles reached to take his hand and then hugged him. Mr. Turner could not help but smile at the relief plastered across Miles's face. Miles had the ring in his pocket, so he showed Mr. Turner who was impressed and appreciated the fact it was a family heirloom piece. Ava would be blown away.

They continued walking past the barn, past the pool and garden area to where the cottage was located. Then turned heading back towards the house. Rob split off to find Anita to share the news; and Miles went to locate Ava who was enjoying a piece of pumpkin pie with an abundant amount of whipped cream.

Sebastian drove at a quick pace towards the airport. He could not wait to drop Daria off so he could head back to the party. He only hoped everyone would still be there by the time he returned. He circled around to her drop off area, then put the car in park, popped the trunk and got her small carryon bag out for her. She snatched it out of his hands, blew him a kiss and said "Ciao" as she sprinted to her gate. *You're welcome. Never again! This was the last time Daria. Ciao.* He got back into the BMW driving with purposed back towards Mapleton.

Natasha was the first to leave and thanked the Petersen's profusely for having her over. They hugged and she told Miles she would see him in the morning. The rest of the guests settled in either the den or back in the billiards room. The Turners, Petersen's and Weston's were all getting along so well, you would have thought they had all been friends for years. Anita Turner had relaxed immensely since arriving, and her husband for one was thrilled. She could be a little high strung lately and he was not used to that, it seemed the older she got, the more she needed to feel in control. He was happy to see her relax and enjoy herself. It was like the old Anita he fell in love with was back.

She took the news remarkably well when he told her Miles had asked him for Ava's hand and was going to ask her to marry him. Rob fully expected her to protest or object, but there was none. Now they would all just have to sit back and wait for him to propose. They had little doubt that Ava would accept, and wondered when they might set a date.

Finally the evening was coming to an end, Maggie left next since she and Candace had a very early morning ahead of them with Black Friday looming. The Turners were the next to leave, and they all hugged planning to do dinner again in a couple of days before Rob had to go back to Wisconsin. Miles stated that he would bring Ava home shortly. Max and Ellen hung out with the family for a while longer getting the Petersen's caught up on the family and horse news. Sebastian finally showed up and was disappointed that he had missed most of the party guests, Maggie in particular. He sulked in the kitchen alone, consoling himself with a cup of coffee and a piece of pie.

Ava followed Miles up to the cottage and sat on the sofa in front of the fire place. Miles turned on the gas logs and returned to her side.

"Well how do you think things went today?" He asked eagerly.

"Oh Miles, everything was lovely. The food was fabulous and everyone seemed to get along so very well."

"I know. I think it all went really well. Ava, I asked your father for your hand tonight and for his blessing."

"What?" She said almost breathless.

"He gave me his blessing. Ava, I would marry you tonight if we could, but you have been through so much lately that I am willing to wait until you feel ready. If you want to wait for six months or a year or more it's completely up to you, I just want you to feel comfortable. I know that I almost lost you once and I do not want to waste another minute." He stated emotionally.

"Well....Are you going to ask me?" She said with a grin.

"Yes. Of course." He grinned. "Ava Elizabeth Turner, will you please marry me?" He stated getting down on one knee, grabbing ahold of her hand.

"Miles Alexander Petersen, I would be honored." With that answer, he leaned in and kissed her. He sat back on the couch and they kissed again. Still holding onto her hand he reached in his pocket then pulled out the box with the ring in it and handed it to her. She opened it slowly and gasped when she saw the exquisite pear shaped diamond. Miles was pleased with her response and lifted the ring out to slide it on her slender delicate finger. Amazingly it fit almost perfectly. He proceeded to tell her the story of the ring and Ava was humbled to receive such a precious family gift.

Chapter 16

Your space or mine?

The next morning arrived and it was as though a town crier had made the announcement of their engagement. Everyone was talking about it and they were the buzz at the local water coolers. Miles was stunned at how many people knew and were congratulating him, since it was only nine thirty in the morning. Life in a small town! Maggie and Candy were in full wedding planning mode talking themes, bridesmaid's dresses, flowers, food and he wasn't convinced the bride had even been consulted. He was overjoyed she had said yes and could not wait until they were actually married, although no date had been set.

Black Friday lived up to its reputation and the La Noel was slammed all day long. The Café was also at capacity and there was no sign that the crowds were slowing down. It was wonderful to see so many people staying in town to shop supporting the local merchants. Maggie and Candace had a system that was working really well with Candace running boxes and wrapping with Maggie on the register. Around noon Anita came and brought the girls lunch and stayed to help with the crowd while they inhaled their food. Ava was dying to come out to help at the store but all the Thanksgiving activities had worn her out. She laid in bed daydreaming about what her wedding might look like as she poured over the calendar looking at months and dates.

There was so much to take into consideration. The businesses, their busy seasons, inventory etc... who could they leave the businesses with while they go on their honeymoon? Did she want a winter wonderland wedding, spring garden or summer beach front wedding? So many options to consider, she had already picked out the style of dress she wanted years ago and time had not changed her taste or her mind. It was a white A-line/Princess square neckline with a court train, made out of Organza with cap sleeves and lace beading wedding dress. It was simple, elegant and best of all affordable. Affordable being key. She had a magazine clipping of the dress that she kept in her jewelry box and couldn't wait to show her mom. Maggie was so ecstatic when Ava called last night to tell her Miles had proposed, she probably didn't sleep a wink the rest of the night.

Candace ran to lock the front door of the La Noel at 8:05 p.m. She and Maggie both collapsed on the fainting sofa letting out a huge sigh, they were exhausted. Black Friday had been a success! When Maggie had checked the register at 6:30 they were already at fifty two hundred dollars. Which was five hundred dollars more than what they did last year on Black Friday and they still had an hour and a half to go. Ava would be thrilled. Miles came by to check on them, and offered to take them out for Mexican since they had worked such a grueling day. They finished closing up, straightened up a few things and then bolted out the door.

Miles called Ava and told her he was taking the girls to supper, so he was going to swing by and pick her up. She loved that he was always so thoughtful thinking of the gals and how hard they had worked all day. She readied herself waiting near the front door for him to arrive. Maggie couldn't wait to drop off the deposit at Ava's, nearly bursting to tell her how well they had done for the day. They were exhausted but happy and still running off adrenaline. Even though Candy looked like a beautiful wilted flower, she still talked non-stop. Miles felt like that might subside once the chips and salsa came out. Or one could hope.

Descending on Ava's doorstep they all started screeching when she opened the door. Maggie screamed out the final number then they started to jump up and down laughing and dancing. Miles just stood there shaking his head.

"Let's go eat ladies!" He encouraged.

"Ok, Ok..." they all chimed in chorus.

They all piled into the Rover and he made his way to the restaurant. Most of the crowd had died down so they were seated quickly. Miles was right, as soon as the chips and salsa arrived at the table Candy went silent, a broad victory smile broke out across his handsome face. The ladies chatted all through dinner often talking at the same time and over each other, so Miles just tried to stay out of the line of fire, and keep track of who was saying what. After about thirty minutes of being lost, he decided to focus on his dinner and gaze at his lovely fiancé. *My, that has a fabulous ring to it...fiancé.*

After all their bellies were full, everyone kind of hit the wall and started to wind down. Miles figured he had better get them all home quickly before he had to carry everyone inside. Tomorrow was another day and an early one for him. Candace would get to sleep in late as they were opening La Noel at the regular time. He still had to get up at four thirty to open the Café by six a.m. He dropped Maggie off at her car then took Ava home, he walked her to the door and tenderly kissed her before watching her go inside.

Miles was half way home before he realized it was silent in the car, as he looked over Candace was sound asleep in the passenger seat. He couldn't help but smile, she really did look sweet and he had a flashback of a car trip their families had taken to Washington D.C. one summer when she was about seven years old. She looked very much like the child version of Candace he remembered. He almost hated to wake her once they arrived at the estate, but he couldn't leave her in the Rover in the middle of winter. Thankfully she stirred once he parked at the cottage, so he was spared having to wake her. She thanked Miles for supper then sleepily stumbled her way into the main house. He entered the cottage and took a quick shower, then he let Zelda inside, who had made her way to the cottage and stood outside barking until he came to the door.

He was almost asleep when his phone rang. "Hello?"

"Did I wake you?" Sebastian inquired.

"Almost...I'm working again so it's back up at four thirty. Is everything ok?"

"I'm sorry that was thoughtless of me. We can talk later. Get some rest."

"Sebastian, it's ok. What's going on?"

"I heard you proposed to Ava. I just wanted to say congratulations."

"Thank you, but you sound as though you have lost your best friend."

"I'm sorry. I don't mean to, I am very happy for you Miles. Truly I am...do you have it all planned out? Date and all of that?"

"Not really, not yet. Maggie and Candace may have it all wrapped up but as far as I know no date has been set. However, we may need to double check with them to be sure." He said with a laugh.

"Oh ok. Well if you need anything just let me know."

"Yeah sure, of course. Sebastian, are you sure you are ok?"

"Yes. I'm sorry I'll catch up with you tomorrow, it's late and you need to get some sleep. Good night."

He hung up before Miles could say anything else. What a strange conversation. There was definitely something going on with Sebastian, but he would have to investigate more tomorrow when he was clear and fully awake.

Sebastian sat alone on his couch in the dark inside his apartment with only the flicker of the gas logs in the fireplace to illuminate his presence. He felt quite miserable and he wasn't sure why. The engagement was expected and he was sincerely thrilled for them both even though his tone tonight did not convey that sentiment. His insides felt hollow like something was eating at him, stealing his sleep. The faux flames mesmerized him and he found himself in that same spot two hours later. Finally he drifted off to sleep in front of the dancing flames.

When he woke the next morning he was stiff and sore from sleeping on the stylish but uncomfortable couch. He dressed in his running attire and hit the road for a quick five mile run. Perhaps that would clear his head, he also wanted—no needed to talk to Maggie and decided he would call her after his run.

Ava decided to surprise Miles and showed up at the Café around ten a.m. He grabbed them a table in the corner then brought her a hot chocolate.

"Miles when do you want to get married? Do you want a big wedding or small? I really need some feedback from you."

"Today, and small." He stated grinning. She squinted her eyes, then swatted at him.

"Seriously. I mean what does your family expect? A huge event? Or do they care? I want to be sensitive to them too, you have an enormous extended family in Boston."

"Sweetheart, they just want to be invited. They will be happy with whatever we want to do. They are pretty laid back when it comes to stuff like this, really."

"Well honestly, I'd like to get married at our church and have a small reception there, but I know that with all the people we know, plus your parent's guest list that we will completely pack out the church and reception hall."

"Mother actually mentioned something to me the other day, but she didn't want to step on toes… so she didn't come directly to you with this idea, but it might work? She was thinking, depending on when the date was set to have a small intimate wedding at the church with a small reception at the fellowship hall. We leave for our honeymoon, and a week or so after we get back have a large reception that they would host in the city for us. Some friends of theirs had a son that eloped, so they did that for him and his wife. It was really nice and worked out great. It's a thought anyway."

"Yeah, I actually kind of like that idea. Regarding dates I have put tons of thought into this trying to find the perfect date. I like this coming February 28th it's the last Saturday in February. I know it's coming up soon, but it gets us past the holidays and inventory. It's before your birthday in May, and mine in October and it's clear of my holiday crazy season. Not to mention we can vacation some place sunny to escape all this snowy cold weather for a week. What do you think?"

"I love it."

"Really? So we have a date?" she said almost giddy.

"I think we do!" Reaching across the table and squeezing her hand. "Should we turn Mags and Candy loose on this thing? If we do, I promise all you will have to do is show up. They will take care of it all." He said sporting his infamous Petersen smile.

"I would if only I could be sure that Maggie wouldn't show up in the lime green taffeta bridesmaid's dress she found like new at the Goodwill store. She's been begging for a place to wear it." She said, and they both busted out laughing.

Sebastian, Mary Beth and Thomas Petersen arrived at the Café immediately zeroing in on Miles and Ava.

"I'm so please we found you two together." Thomas started.

"Dad, Mom, hi. Wow, well this is a pleasure. I wasn't expecting to see you." Miles stated nervously and looked over at Sebastian confused. Soon Maggie walked in to joined them and now Ava and Miles were looking at each other as though an intervention was about to take place.

"Your brother and Maggie have been up to some devious things these past few weeks, so I wanted to show you first-hand what they have been up to in your absence." Thomas continued. Sebastian looked like the Cheshire cat and Maggie was barely able to hold it together trying to maintain a straight face.

"Please, all of you…walk with me." Thomas stated firmly. He walked back to an area to the left of the Barista station that was covered with a heavy tarp. Miles had been told that someone had accidently damaged the wall and it was being repaired so they kept it covered to keep the drywall dust down in the Café. He was so distracted with Ava getting better that he had not questioned it. Plus he knew Sebastian was dealing with getting it fixed. With dramatic flair Thomas ripped the tarp down exposing the new entry way into the expanded seating area of the Café complete with the overstuffed furniture that Miles had picked out months ago.

There was an audible gasp from both Miles and Ava as they looked stunned at each other along with the crowd that now surrounded them. Maggie was ecstatic, all but jumping up and down and Sebastian was grinning from ear to ear.

"I got the space?" Miles said softly. Then looking at Sebastian tearing up he said "You did all this? For me?"

"You both got the space! We have done a few things for Lady Ava too, dear brother." Sebastian reached over and hugged Miles then patted him on the back. Thomas and Mary Beth were beaming with pride.

Your space or mine?

Ava stood there in shock with her hand over her mouth. Maggie grabbed her and drug her into the new area to show her all around, then she walked her back towards the new restrooms for the Café. Back there was a hidden locked sliding pocket door that joined the two spaces allowing you to enter from the Café into the La Noel. She unlocked it revealing the new public bathrooms for the La Noel then led her up the hallway to the new enormous storage area for the store. Maggie and Candy had worked diligently moving boxes and rearranging everything, shifting things in the store for maximum storage and display space.

Ava burst into happy tears of relief and joy as she looked around the new room, it was amazing.

The Petersen's quickly caught up to the women who were standing there taking it all in. Miles once again shook his dad's hand thanking him, then hugged his mother and Sebastian once more.

"Thank you for doing this Sebastian, and thank you for what you have done for Ava. This is fantastic, so much better than I could have ever imagined. So Candy knew about all this?" He asked in amazement.

"Amazing, right? Probably the first secret she has ever kept in her life!" Sebastian said laughing. He caught Maggie's eye and winked at her. They had pulled off the surprise!

Miles made his way over to Ava lifting her up and spinning her around. "Look at all your space sweetheart! What do you think?" He set her down gently keeping a hand on her to hold her steady. She looked at everything one more time then walked over to Thomas and gave him a great big hug. Then she spotted Sebastian kind of hanging back a bit, she grabbed him and looked into his eyes. She leaned up and kissed his cheek then whispered in his ear, "This is all so lovely and I truly thank you from the bottom of my heart. Well done Sebastian. Well done." Sebastian kissed her back on the cheek then gave her a warm hug. Grabbing his hand and walking him back over to where Miles, Maggie and his parents were standing; Ava encouraged him to say something.

"I am so pleased with the way the space turned out, and I could not have accomplished any of this without my fantastic partner in crime, Miss Maggie Willis." Sebastian announced. Everyone started clapping so Maggie took a dramatic bow.

"Working on this project with Sebastian for the two of you guys was truly a labor of love for me, and we had a great time doing it. He can be my partner anytime!" Maggie said smiling glancing over at Sebastian who was grinning and gave her a nod. They seemed to be back on track. Whatever track that was she wasn't quite sure, but happy that they could at the very least be friends.

The next few weeks were a flurry of activity between work, church, Christmas cantatas, premarital counseling and wedding plans. Christmas was magical with snow flurries on Christmas Eve and everyone she loved in town for the holidays. Time was spent visiting and making wedding plans with the Petersen's. Miles bought Ava the Toyota Highlander she had looked at earlier in the month and she found it sitting in the driveway Christmas morning with a big red bow. She had no idea Miles was giving her that and although she had protested at first, she was elated to have received it. Miraculously all the women, Mary Beth, Anita, Ava, Maggie and Candace all were in sync in regards to the wedding plans, that Miles and Ava set forth regarding the wedding and reception afterwards. Power of serious prayer Ava surmised.

The wedding date was set, and the date was reserved at the church. The wedding party was selected and their attire had been determined. The flowers, food and reception decorations were all selected so now they just had to wait for the date to arrive. Ava was able to find her dream dress in the city, and since it was out of season, the price was discounted which made it well within her budget. A few alterations had to be made to take it in at the waist and hem it, but other than that it was perfect making her look angelic in it.

The Petersen family had a lovely house in Pembroke, Bermuda located on the north shore so that is where Miles was taking Ava for their honeymoon. The Petersen's usually went to the Bermuda house during the summer months to recharge their batteries and they allow other family members or friends to use the house throughout the year. Thomas made sure the private jet was ready and the first two weeks in March were clear for the newlyweds.

Finally their special day had arrived, the church was filled to capacity with family and friends. Candace was at the helm as the wedding coordinator and so far everything was going smoothly according to plan. The flowers were exquisite, the reception area for a church fellowship hall had been transformed with crisp white table cloths covering long and round tables with dark purple accents and purple and yellow tulips everywhere. An ice sculpture stood in one corner near where the beverage table was located. The cake was a four tier beauty with smooth white fondant and a thin purple ribbon that circled the bottom of each later with fresh purple and yellow tulips strategically placed. The caterers were dressed all in black pants and crisp white shirts with black bow ties and were all in place ready to serve.

The church had a wide center aisle and Miles along with his father as the best man, stood waiting at the altar with Pastor Mark. The grandparents had been seated and the mothers were now in place so it was time for the bridesmaids to walk down the aisle. Sebastian was paired with Maggie, who looked regal in her floor length dark purple square cut neck A-line dress holding yellow tulips in her bouquet. The men all had on black tuxedos with a purple vest and bowtie except for Miles whose vest was charcoal with a black bow tie.

Sebastian could not take his eyes off her, she looked elegant and amazing. He winked and smiled at her as she took his arm then they walked slowly down the aisle. Next up was Ava's cousin Karen, who was paired with Miles's best friend Max. The flower girl and ring bearer were three year old fraternal twins of friends who attended their church. They were absolutely adorable and everyone ooh'ed and awed as they walked down the aisle throwing flower petals and waving at people they knew from the crowd.

The beautiful dramatic music started, so everyone stood as the large double doors in the back of the church swung open to reveal the bride. She looked heavenly with her hair swept up in an elegant up doo held in place with a faux diamond clip with loose curls strategically escaping around her face and neck. She wore a diamond necklace that Mary Beth let her borrow with petite tear drop diamond earrings that Maggie and Candace had gone in together on as a wedding shower gift. Her bouquet was a simple one that matched the bridesmaids except hers consisted of both the purple and yellow tulips tied with white ribbon.

Ava looked as though she were gliding as she was walking down the aisle, taking Miles's breath away the closer she got to him. Pastor Mark began the ceremony by opening in prayer, and by the time he was finished, the songs sung and vows spoken there was not a dry eye in the sanctuary. Miles and Ava were so sweet and tender with one another so anyone who knew them and what they had been through, wished them nothing but love, joy and contentment.

Miles was convinced Pastor Mark would never get to the *kiss* part, so when he finally gave the charge Ava looked up at Miles with her big blue eyes, and he gently but passionately kissed her. When they faced forward holding hands and the Pastor presented them as Mr. and Mrs. Miles Alexander Petersen for the first time, the church erupted with clapping and cheers.

Joy radiated from the couple as they took their first steps down the aisle as husband and wife. Miles looked lovingly over at Ava, his heart swelling with pride. He knew deep in his soul that no matter what they faced as a couple in their marriage that between their love, faith and keeping God in the center of their lives that there was nothing they could not work through together. Indeed this was not the fairytale book ending that little girls dream of, but it was a new beginning ordained by God, which was even better.

THE END

CPSIA information can be obtained at www.ICGtesting.com
Printed in the USA
LVOW04s1345051214

417385LV00014B/227/P

9 781498 405324